The VNR Concise Guide to
ACCOUNTING
AND CONTROL

VNR CONCISE MANAGEMENT SERIES

The VNR Concise Guide to
ACCOUNTING
AND CONTROL

VNR CONCISE MANAGEMENT SERIES

Edited by

Carl Heyel

 VAN NOSTRAND REINHOLD COMPANY
NEW YORK   CINCINNATI   ATLANTA   DALLAS   SAN FRANCISCO
LONDON   TORONTO   MELBOURNE

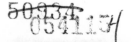

Van Nostrand Reinhold Company Regional Offices:
New York   Cincinnati   Atlanta   Dallas   San Francisco

Van Nostrand Reinhold Company International Offices:
London   Toronto   Melbourne

Copyright © 1979 by Litton Educational Publishing, Inc.

Library of Congress Catalog Card Number: 78-18365
ISBN: 0-442-23407-4

Manufactured in the United States of America

Published by Van Nostrand Reinhold Company
135 West 50th Street, New York. N.Y. 10020

Published simultaneously in Canada by Van Nostrand Reinhold Ltd.

15 14 13 12 11 10 9 8 7 6 5 4 3 2 1

Library of Congress Cataloging in Publication Data

Main entry under title:

VNR concise guide to accounting and
    control.

    (VNR concise management series)
    Includes index.
    1. Managerial accounting.   2. Cost accounting.
I. Heyel, Carl, 1908–
HF5635.V26   658.1′511   78-18365
ISBN 0-442-23407-4

CARL HEYEL, *Editor*

Management Counsel, Manhasset, New York, and editor, *The Encyclopedia of Management*
Formerly Adjunct Professor, Industrial Management and Industrial Marketing, The Polytechnic Institute of Brooklyn

DR. L. J. BENNINGER, *Advisory Editor, Accounting Subjects*

Professor of Accounting, University of Florida, Gainesville, Florida

DANIEL F. O'DONNELL, *Advisory Editor, Depreciation*

O'Donnell Sales & Engineering, Inc., Buffalo, New York

VNR CONCISE MANAGEMENT SERIES

This volume of the Van Nostrand Reinhold Concise Management Series, as are all of its companion volumes, is for those executives and potential executives who find that they have to broaden their horizons beyond their own specialties if they are to advance in management. To this end, it has been edited to meet the needs of the person who seeks to acquire a grounding in the basic concepts of a management discipline foreign to his or her area of expertise, but who does not have the time or desire to plow through the detailed expositions and practice exercises in books edited for practitioners. At the same time, the volumes in the Series serve as admirable references and "concept updaters" for those professionally trained in the fields covered.

The chapters in each volume have been prepared by experts in the subject matter covered, and originally appeared as entries in the best-seller Heyel *Encyclopedia of Management*, also published by Van Nostrand Reinhold. However, all of the entries have been revised and updated by Mr. Heyel as required, in collaboration with the original authors, the indicated advisory editors, and other recognized authorities.

Acknowledgments

As indicated in our opening statement, the chapters in this volume, which appeared originally in *The Encyclopedia of Management*, have been updated and revised as necessary. Special recognition is due Dr. L. J. Benninger, who contributed four of the accounting entries in the Encyclopedia and advised on all accounting-related entries in addition to those of his own authorship. Original Encyclopedia authorships and affiliations are as follows:

1. Management Accounting: W. B. McFarland, Ph.D., Lecturer in Accounting, California State College, Hayward, Calif; formerly Director of Research, National Association of Accountants, New York, N.Y. 2. Organizational Responsibilities: J. L. Peirce, Vice President–Finance, A.B. Dick Company, Chicago, Ill., for Financial Executives Institute, New York, N.Y. 3. Cash Flow Analysis: W. B. McFarland. 4. Break-Even Analysis: Winfield Hutton, Hunter College of the City University of New York, N.Y. and J. T. Powers, Peat, Marwick, Mitchell & Co., New York, N.Y. 5. Cost Accounting: L. J. Benninger, Ph.D., Professor of Accounting, University of Florida, Gainesville, Fla. 6. Standard Costing: L. J. Benninger. 7. Cost Control: L. J. Benninger. 8. Overhead Assignment: Phil Carroll, Industrial Engineer, Maplewood, N.J. 9. Depreciation: Daniel F. O'Donnell, O'Donnell Sales & Engineering, Inc., Buffalo, N.Y. 10. Budgeting: L. J. Benninger. 11. Direct (Variable) Costing: W. B. McFarland. 12. Statistical Accounting: C. E. Graese, C.P.A., Partner, Peat, Marwick, Mitchell & Co., New York, N.Y. 13. Marketing Cost Analysis: Michael

Schiff, Ph.D., Ross Professor of Accounting, Graduate School of Business Administration, New York University, New York, N.Y. 14. Industrial Research Accounting: W. B. McFarland. 15. Industrial Research Budgeting: W. B. McFarland. 16. Internal Auditing: Archie McGhee, Institute of Internal Auditors, Winter Park, Fla. 17. Credit Management: Robert D. Goodwin, Executive Vice President, National Association of Credit Management, New York, N.Y. 18. Credit Reporting: Dun & Bradstreet, New York, N.Y. 19. Individual Credit and Collections: John L. Spafford, President, Associated Credit Bureaus, Inc., Houston, Texas.

Introduction

Accounting has been defined by the American Accounting Association as "the process of identifying, measuring, and communicating economic information to permit informed judgments and decisions by users of the information." This process is usually organized as a system of techniques and procedures which covers an entity (business enterprise, governmental unit, etc.) and generates information on resources that are susceptible to measurement in financial terms.

The purpose is to meet the need for such information by managers (owners) and others (investors, creditors, government, etc.). Consequently, there are two basic sets of accounting reports—*internal* and *external*. Internal reporting is designed in accordance with directly identifiable specific management requirements, while external reporting is governed by "generally accepted accounting principles," which are conventions or rules developed to assure reliable information required to fulfill management's fiduciary responsibilities to others.

This volume of the VNR Concise Management Series is oriented to accounting concepts primarily involved in the daily operations of the business, as distinguished from the longer-range corporate financing and related matters which are treated in the companion volume, "VNR Concise Guide to Financial Management." However, there are a number of accounting-related and financial-related concepts of interest both to the executive concerned with continuing operating controls, and the executive whose primary concern is with problems of corporate financing, investment decisions, and long-range financial planning. Accordingly, to make each volume logically complete, an editorial decision was made to have several chapters appear identically in each—although they will, of course, be read with a different orientation in mind.

Top organizational responsibility for accounting control and financial planning rests in the two positions of Controller and Treasurer, although these titles may sometimes be augmented by the designation as vice president, and the incumbents may report to a financial vice president.

By and large, controllership is concerned primarily with the concepts and techniques treated in the present volume, and treasurership with those covered in Financial Management. However, practice is not uniform, and certain reponsibilities may be subsumed under either. Chapter 2 presents a description of both functions.

MANAGEMENT ACCOUNTNG VS. PUBLIC ACCOUNTING

Two major fields of accounting practice may be distinguished: (1) *management accounting* and (2) *public accounting*. The management accountant performs accounting services as an employee or officer of the enterprise. The public accountant's primary functions are independent auditing and reporting on financial statements. Most public accountants have met statutory requirements for practice as a Certified Public Accountant (CPA). These requirements are set by the American Institute of Certified Public Accountants, the national organization of CPAs. Each CPA has the responsibility for conducting his examination in accordance with generally accepted auditing standards and for stating in his report, among other things, whether the financial statement of an enterprise is presented in accordance with generally accepted accounting principles. With respect to management accounting, the National Association of Accountants, as indicated in Chapter 1 herein, issues a Certified Management Accountant (CMA) certificate in recognition of educational attainment and professional competency.

Since this book is concerned with management accounting, responsibilities and activities of certified public accountants are covered in the companion volume on financial management.

Contents

The VNR Concise Guide to
ACCOUNTING AND CONTROL

VNR CONCISE MANAGEMENT SERIES

1

Management Accounting

Management accounting is concerned with supplying financial data useful to management at all levels in planning and administering an enterprise. More specifically, three different areas can be distinguished in which management has need for financial data provided by the accountant, *viz:*

(1) In long and short range strategic planning there is need for evaluating alternatives in financial terms.

(2) In administering operations, management needs to know promptly when current results deviate significantly from planned results.

(3) In discharging management's obligation to report on the results of its stewardship to stockholders, creditors, and others having a legitimate interest in financial operations of the enterprise.

While management accounting has been most highly developed in profit-oriented businesses, there is need for reliable financial data to guide operation of any enterprise that employs economic resources.

The uses listed above cover a wide variety of individual purposes for which accounting data may be used. An equally wide range exists in the kinds of data relevant to these purposes and in the techniques employed to measure and to communicate the data. However, many of these techniques are comparatively recent.

EVOLUTION OF MANAGEMENT ACCOUNTING

In the past, the accountant's function was restricted to recording financial transactions and preparing periodic summaries of financial position and income. The resulting historical record served an important purpose, but it gave little assistance in planning future operations or in directing current operations toward realization of plans. This inadequacy was most serious at divisional and departmental levels, for accounting services were seldom available and the accountant's reports had little relevance to problems faced by management at these levels.

The Scientific Management movement aroused a widespread demand for reliable quantitative data to guide management actions, and accounting was swept into the stream in the early years of the twentieth century. In the process, the management accountant's outlook has broadened to include the present and the future as well as the past, and accounting has become an integral part of modern management technology. While accounting is a staff function, the management accountant now exercises a substantial influence on decisions through selection and interpretation of data. As a result he is, in effect, an active participant in management.

The process began in Cost Accounting, with the introduction of Standard Costing. Every supervisor having authority to incur costs could be appraised in terms of his current performance relative to pre-established standard costs.

With the development of budgeting, the same concept of forward financial planning was extended to cover *all* operations during a chosen period of time. In a complete application, a budget is a coordinated financial plan for operations summarized in statements of income and financial position for the budget period. Management is thus in a position to see in advance the expected results of its operating plans and to make changes in these plans if it believes the results can be improved.

In historical reporting, the accountant is concerned only with those events which have occurred; but in developing data to guide management *planning*, he must consider the entire range of alternatives from which management chooses in making decisions. Since volume or level of activity is usually a significant independent variable, techniques for measuring functional relationships between cost, volume, and profit have been extensively developed.

Continuing and systematic analysis of cost-volume-profit relationships is obtained through *Flexible Budgets* and *Direct Costing*. Special studies following the marginal approach are used in non-repetitive situations. Special cost and income construction are also prepared to reflect changes in variables other than volume (e.g. prices of cost factors, production methods, mix, selling prices).

Analytical techniques for evaluating and comparing alternatives are now widely employed in conjuction with the preparation of budgets. Termed *Profit Planning*, the variable factors are manipulated to find a combination which promises an acceptable financial outcome. Criteria such as rate of return on capital employed, sales volume, and share of the market are used to judge acceptability of a proposed plan. (These matters are covered in the companion volume on financial management.)

ORGANIZATION OF THE MANAGEMENT ACCOUNTING FUNCTION

Within an enterprise, broad responsibility for the accounting function is usually assigned to the Controller, although other titles are common. In a large organization, sub-functions such as the following are recognized.

Financial Accounting. Accounting for revenues, expenses, assets, liabilities, and net worth together with the production of summary financial reports.

Cost Accounting. Accounting for current, standard, and prospective costs; analysis and communication of cost data at all levels of management within the organization.

Systems and Procedures design and installation.

Data Processing. Recording accounting data, performing repetitive operations with these data (e.g. payroll preparation), preparing reports from recorded data.

Internal Auditing. Review and appraisal of accounting procedures and records to ascertain their reliability, conformance with prescribed practices, and adequacy to protect against loss of assets by fraud, waste, and other causes.

Budgeting. Assembly and consolidation of budgets; assistance to management personnel in translating operating plans into financial budgets; reporting and analysis of budget variances.

Tax Reporting. Preparing reports required by Federal, state and local tax authorities.

Financial Analysis. Interpretation of accounting reports: analysis in financial terms of proposed projects, plans, and procedures; assistance to management in interpretation and evaluation of financial data of all types.

CERTIFIED MANAGEMENT ACCOUNTANT (CMA)

The National Association of Accountants began a new certification program in 1972 designed to recognize educational attainment and professional competency. Unlike the CPA certificate for public accountants which is granted by a particular state, the Certified Management Accountant (CMA) certificate is given by the Association. Basically the program consists of four phases: (1) meeting one of the conditions to sit for the CMA examination; (2) taking a comprehensive, five-part written examination; (3) securing the requisite personal recommendations; and (4) once the certificate has been earned, meeting the annual continuing education requirements. The last-named requirement calls for the holder of the certificate to engage in 30 hours a year of professional study.

Subjects covered in the five-part written examination (only two of which need be taken at one time) are:

(1) Economics and business finance.
(2) Organization and behavior, including ethical considerations.
(3) Public reporting standards, auditing, and taxes.
(4) Periodic reporting for internal and external purposes.
(5) Decision analysis, including modelling and information systems. Passing this part customarily demands some familiarity with the computer.

The CMA program has been an outstanding success, and the earning of the CMA certificate has become a "must" for the professional who specializes in management accounting.

2

Organizational Responsibilities

As stated in the introduction, top organizational responsibility for financial planning and control rests in the two positions of Controller and Treasurer, although these titles may sometimes be augmented by the designation as vice president, and the incumbents may report to a financial vice president.

By and large, controllership is concerned primarily with the concepts and techniques treated in the present volume, and treasurership with those covered in the companion volume, "Financial Management." However, practice is not uniform, and certain responsibilities may be subsumed under either. Following are descriptions of both functions.

CONTROLLERSHIP

Controllership is the function of business management which combines the responsibility for accounting, reporting, budgeting, measurement, operating controls, auditing, taxes and related areas. It is based on the word "control"—not in the direct sense of the control exercised by stockholders, corporate presidents, or operating executives, but in the indirect or "functional" sense that it provides and coordinates mechanism for controlling action and making decisions with profit objectives in mind. Budgetary control is perhaps the purest example of the controllership principle in ordinary practice, but the latter includes all forms of measurement and appraisal. The function is typically performed by an executive with the title of Controller, but is frequently assigned, totally or in part, to a financial vice president or a treasurer, or divided in various ways between executives with other titles. It is closely allied to the planning function.

Formal Definition.   An authoritative definition has been published for many years by the Financial Executives Institute (formerly Controllers Institute of America). The Institute's concept of the function of controllership is:

(1) *Planning for Control.* To establish, coordinate, and administer, as an integral part of management, an adequate plan for the control of operations. Such a plan would provide, to the extent required in the business, profit planning, programs for capital investing and for financing, sales forecasts, expense budgets, and cost standards, together with the necessary procedures to effectuate the plan.

(2) *Reporting and Interpreting.* To compare performance with operating plans and standards, and to report and interpret the results of operations to all levels of management and to the owners of the business. This function includes the formulation of accounting policy, the coordination of systems and procedures, and the preparation of operating data and special reports as required.

(3) *Evaluating and Consulting.* To consult with all segments of management responsible for policy or action concerning any phase of the operation of the business as it relates to the attainment of objectives and the effectiveness of policies, organization structure, and procedures.

(4) *Tax Administration.* To establish and administer tax policies and procedures.

(5) *Government Reporting.* To supervise or coordinate the preparation of reports to government agencies.

(6) *Protection of Assets.* To assure protection for the assets of the business through internal control, internal auditing, and assuring proper insurance coverage.

(7) *Economic Appraisal.* To appraise continuously the economic and social forces and government influences, and to interpret their effect upon the business.

Spelling. The terms "controller" and "comptroller" are identical in meaning. The former is the more modern form and is gradually becoming universal, although the by-laws many large corporations still provide the older title. The word "comptroller" is associated by lexicographers with the French word *compte* (account) or with *compt*, the keeper of a counter-roll or check list.

History. Controllership grew from the increased demands on accountants in the decade of the twenties. The accounting science, which had received strong impetus from the first U.S. income tax law (1913), was challenged during the depression of 1930–33 to contribute directly to profit planning. Controllers Institute of America was founded in 1913, to offer controllers of medium and large size companies a means for exchanging ideas and developing the science of controllership in business management. This group was primarily responsible for establishing the title of Controller as a recognized corporate office. In 1962, recognizing the integration with capital procuring, investment, and other money management functions which had progressively been identifying the interests of controllers, treasurers, and financial vice presidents, the organization changed its name to Financial Executives Institute. By 1978 it had grown to a membership of 10,000, with 68 chapters throughout the United States, Puerto Rico, and Canada.

Controllership principles, organizationally centered in a single executive, have come to be widely used (though with considerable variations in practice) in the United States and Canada, and are now beginning to command attention in other countries.

Related Techniques. Controllership is most closely related to accounting—particularly cost accounting—and to budgeting, subjects which have their own individual development, literature, and professional organizations. At management level, these, together with auditing and taxes, are commonly treated as segments of the controllership responsibility. The techiques of money management (embracing capital procurement, investment and so on) are also closely allied, though properly the concern of Treasurership. Controllers are often involved in the techniques of electronic data processing, and more recently in the development of management information systems (MIS) to provide selected decision-oriented information needed by management to plan, control, and evaluate the activities of the corporation. They are also involved in the systems and procedures function, in the sense of designing, installing, and coordinating paperwork flow and the like, although this group of functions may be assigned elsewhere so long as the needs of control are served.

A specialized management function is planning, which is vital to controllership since there can be no control without planning. However, most informed opinion holds that controllers should not be responsible for planning, although its *modus operandi* is their major concern. The term "management planning and control" emphasizes the involvement of controllership with planning.

TREASURERSHIP

Treasurership is the function of business management which combines the responsibility for the custody and investment of money, the granting of credit and collection of accounts, the provision of capital, the maintenance of a market for the company's securities, and related areas. Although essentially charged with all of the duties which fall under the heading of "money management," perhaps the most challenging aspect of treasurership today is creating and maintaining the company's capital structure. Included in this activity is borrowing, both long and short term, and the sale of capital stock issues, as well as the cultivation, through financial public relations, of a market for such securities. Treasurership is closely allied to controllership, but whereas the latter is purely a staff type function, the treasurer is generally endowed with broad authority to take action with respect to banking, disbursement of cash, borrowing, and investing.

Formal Definition. An authoritative definition is published by Financial Executives Institute. The Institute's concept of the function of treasurership is:

(1) *Provison of Capital.* To establish and execute programs for the provision of the capital required by the business, including negotiating the procurement of capital and maintaining the required finanical arrangements.

(2) *Investor Relations.* To establish and maintain an adequate market for the company's securities and, in connection therewith, to maintain adequate liaison with investment bankers, financial analysts, and shareholders.

(3) *Short-term Financing.* To maintain adequate sources for the company's current borrowings from commercial banks and other lending institutions.

(4) *Banking and Custody.* To maintain banking arrangements, to receive, have custody of, and disburse the comany's monies and securities and to be responsible for the financial aspects of real estate transactions.

(5) *Credits and Collections.* To direct the granting of credit and the collection of accounts due the company, including the supervision of required special arrangements for financing sales, such as time payment and leasing plans.

(6) *Investments.* To invest the company's funds as required, and to establish and coordinate policies for investment in pension and other similar trusts.

(7) *Insurance.* To provide insurance coverage as required.

History.   The function of the treasurer is almost as old as recorded history, examples being plentiful in th Bible and other ancient writings. The financial management function has always been recognized as a well defined necessity in business enterprise, requiring specialized training and skills. In recent times, various local treasurers' clubs and associations have been organized, but a milestone in the development of the techniques of treasurership through organization occurred in 1962 when, as indicated earlier, Controllers Institute of America, recognizing its already large representation among the treasurers in the United States, Puerto Rico, and Canada, adopted the name Financial Executives Institute, and began the conscious dedication of its energies to development of treasureship along with controllership.

Related Techniques.   Treasurership is closely related to accounting, to controllership and, in a broader sense, to economics as applied in the field of corporate finance and investment. Specialized phases of corporate activity frequently assigned to the treasurer are insurance, leasing, time payment plans and, tax administration. Credit and collection practice is almost universally his direct responsibility. Some of these subjects have their own literature and professional organizations.

3
Cash Flow Analysis

Cash flow analysis is concerned with the cash phase of the capital turnover cycle. In a going business, the turnover of capital follows a continuous cycle which proceeds from cash to assets such as plant, equipment, and inventory; to receivables; and back to cash. Significant figures which describe the cash phase are (1) cash balance at any given time, and (2) rate of cash flow (inflow, out-flow, net increase or decrease) per unit of time.

REASONS FOR CASH FLOW ANALYSIS

A company must have enough cash to meet obligations as they mature, and management has customarily met this problem by carrying cash balances supplemented by sources of credit which experience has shown to be adequate for the purpose. In recent years, emphasis has been placed on cash flow to guide management in deploying its liquid capital resources most effectively. Financial management has become increasingly aware that, while capital in the form of cash or equivalent assets can earn a return, this rate of return is generally much below the rate that can be earned from investments in other types of business assets. Hence cash balances are held at minimum levels consistent with anticipated requirements in order that cash in excess of such requirements can be promptly invested.

Cash flow has also come into widespread use by investors as an index of management's opportunity to shift a company's capital into areas offering the most attractive rates of return and as a measure of ability to pay dividends when undivided profits are available. Interest in cash flow analysis reflects a business environment characterized by rapid technological change and growth. It also reflects wider divergence between cash flow and periodic net profits as accounting methods have become increasingly affected by tax considerations.

N.A.A. Research Report No. 38 ("Cash Flow Analysis for Managerial Control") defines cash as "capital in the form of cash or equivalent assets available at management's discretion for meeting obligations as they mature or for investment in operating assets." Usually included are temporary investments made to hold cash, provided such investments can be converted to cash without material delay or loss when needed for disbursements. Excluded are assets such as plant, equipment, and inventories which cannot be converted into cash for making current disbursements without impairing future revenues.

The definition above reflects the intent to measure funds available for disbursement in the immediate or near future. Somewhat different definitions are used for other purposes. For example, when the purpose is to measure funds available for capital expenditures, the relevant figure is net cash flow after deducting outlays for current operating costs and other recurring disbursements. In statements prepared to describe the flow of funds through a business over a period of time, cash is not always distinguished from other current assets, and certain transactions in which no cash changes hands (e.g. issue of capital stock for assets) may be reported as cash flows. Like many other accounting concepts, cash flow needs to be defined and measured in relation to the purpose for which the resulting data are intended.

CASH FORECASTS

Management needs reliable information about cash balances and cash flow to guide financial planning and current administration of cash assets. Since decisions relate to the future, forecasts of cash movements constitute the principal sources of data for the purpose. Historical data are useful only insofar as they give an insight into the future. Some of the information needed in management of cash may be developed in the processes of budgeting and accounting, but additional procedures are required.

Three distinct patterns are distinguishable in cash forecasts, viz.:

(1) Forecasts of cash receipts and disbursements by days or weeks for periods ranging from one to six weeks ahead. These forecasts show adequacy of cash balances to meet disbursements, guide transfers of cash between company locations and bank accounts, and show how much cash is available for temporary investment on a day-by-day basis. Anticipated cash collections and scheduled disbursements constitute the basic data for these short period forecasts. Ordinarily they are used only by financial management.

(2) Forecasts of cash flows and balances for the coming year by months and quarters. The principal purposes served by monthly forecasts are to disclose periods of cash shortage in time for loans to be arranged and to show when excess cash will be available for temporary investment. Knowing when cash will be available and when it will be needed, investment media and maturities can be selected to obtain the best available yields together with the desired degree of liquidity. Forecasting proceeds by scheduling receipts and disbursements, or, more commonly, by adjusting budgeted income to an approximate cash basis. Exhibit I shows, in summary form, a typical annual forecast of cash receipts and disbursements. Annual cash forecasts are usually a phase of the annual budget.

(3) Long-range forecasts of cash flow covering periods of several years in advance. An N.A.A. research study ("Cash Flow Analysis for Managerial Control") found that five years was the period most commonly used for long-range cash forecasts by 42 companies which participated in the study. Such forecasts serve primarily to indicate amounts and timing of internally generated cash available for capital expenditures or the amounts of additional cash which must be provided to support a given program. The long-range cash forecast is an aspect of over-all long-range financial planning.

EXHIBIT I

CASH FORECAST

Fiscal Year 19.

	November	December	January	February	March	April	May	Totals for Year
Gross Shipments	1200	1987	2063	1387	2363	2325	1575	21000
Cash Balance Beginning of Month	375	396	222	150	257	160	192	375
Add: Cash Receipts								
Collections of Accounts Receivable	1380	1350	1605	1635	1680	2055	2205	19305
Miscellaneous Receipts	66	81	70	105	105	97	97	1050
Total Receipts	1446	1431	1675	1740	1785	2152	2302	20355
Total Cash Available	1821	1827	1897	1890	2042	2312	2494	20730
Less: Cash Disbursements								
Operating Expenses	810	915	1035	885	975	1020	960	10830
Raw Materials Purchases	503	570	1050	600	607	555	345	7140
Taxes	112	60	412	13		395	3	1310
Dividends				135			135	517
Pension Contribution		210						247
Total Disbursements	1425	1755	2497	1633	1582	1970	1443	20044
Cash Balance or (Deficiency) End of Month Before Bank Loans or (Repayments)	396	72	(600)	257	460	342	1051	686
Bank Loans or (Repayments)		150	750		(300)	(150)	(450)	(900)
Cash Balance End of Month	396	222	150	257	160	192	601	686

(From "Cash Flow Analysis for Managerial Control," *N.A.A. Research Report 38*)

CASH FLOW REPORTS

Detailed and frequent reports giving actual bank balances, receipts, disbursements, and transfers are used by financial management as a guide to need for decisions and for revising current forecasts. Top executives responsible for coordinating all functions usually receive frequent summary reports of cash position.

Summary statements intending to show the periodic flow of funds through the reporting entity are commonly included with both internal and external financial reports. These statements vary considerably in form and specific conduct.

In funds statements accompanying published financial reports, the term "funds" most commonly denotes working capital or net

EXHIBIT II

Sources and Uses of Funds	
Year ended December 31, 19__	
(thousands of dollars)	
Cash and marketable securities -- beginning of period	$ 156,109
Funds were made available from:	
Net income before taxes	$ 210,373
Charges against income not requiring current cash outlays (depreciation, depletion, property abandoned, accrued expenses, provision for deferred income taxes)	138,487
Funds generated by operations	$ 348,860
Bank loans	5,260
Capital stock issued	135,360
Miscellaneous -- net	1,282
Total funds made available	$ 490,762
Funds were used for:	
Acquisition, construction and replacement of property, plant, and equipment	$ 243,815
Income taxes	56,070
Dividends	82,870
Investments and advances -- subsidiary companies	7,405
Interest payments and reduction of long-term debt	20,617
Increase in inventories, receivables, and prepaid expenses less amounts payable for purchases, payrolls, taxes, etc.	25,624
Total funds used	$ 436,401
Increase in cash and marketable securities	$ 54,361
Cash and marketable securities -- end of period	$ 210,470

(From "Cash Flow Analysis for Managerial Control," *N.A.A. Research Report 38*)

current assets. However, the N.A.A. study previously cited found that management tends to visualize funds flows as cash flows and prefers statements which relate financial transactions to cash balances rather than working capital balances (see Exhibit II). In these statements, sources of funds received during the period (e.g., earnings, sales of assets, loans, issue of capital stock) are shown as additions to the opening cash balance and applications of funds listed by major categories (e.g., income taxes, interest, dividends, investment in long-lived assets, additions to current assets, repayment of loans) as deductions to arrive at the closing cash balance. Statement form is flexible and may be designed to emphasize desired aspects (e.g., funds available for capital expenditures).

Funds flows so reported are not all cash flows in a narrow sense, but include some transactions (e.g., earnings represented by receivables, property acquired on credit in which cash did not actually change hands). However, these items do reflect purchasing power available for disposition by management and inclusion in the statement helps show how the business was financed during the period.

4

Break-Even Analysis

Break-even analysis, a method for studying the relationships among sales revenue, fixed costs, and variable expenses to determine the minimum volume at which production can be profitable, is a useful technique in business decision-making. The basic break-even model can be adapted to three specific situations that often arise in business analysis:

(1) Multi-product operations.

(2) Variation in selling price, with the related problem of price-output determination.

(3) Mechanization decisions.

The general break-even function is as follows:

$$S = F/(1 - V)$$

where S is the break-even sales volume, F is total fixed costs, and V is the ratio of total variable costs to expected dollar net sales volume.

MULTI-PRODUCT OPERATIONS

Most companies produce more than one product. Thus, there is frequently a need to adapt break-even analysis to multi-product operations and to changes in product mix. As might be expected, the break-even volume varies with the product mix. The greater the proportion of total sales accounted for by the products with higher than average margins, the lower the break-even volume.

A specific example illustrates how variation in product mix can be represented graphically without introducing undue complexities. Assume that a company produces five products (A, B, C, D, and E) with variable cost per cents (V) of 60, 65, 70, 75, and 80, respectively, and total fixed costs (F), of $100,000.

Substitute these different variable cost percentages in the general break-even equation, and calculate five different break-even volumes, assuming successively that each of the products is the only one sold. Plot these five points on a chart (see the lower curve in Exhibit I), with the horizontal axis representing variable cost per cents and the vertical axis representing sales dollars. The resulting curve is a *break-even zone* for product mixes representing all possible combinations of the five products. The break-even zone for this company will be between $250,000 (assuming product A is the only one sold) and $500,000 (assuming product E is the only one sold).

EXHIBIT I

APPLICATION OF BREAK-EVEN ANALYSIS TO
MULTI-PRODUCT OPERATIONS

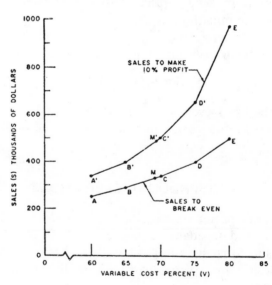

EXHIBIT II

DETERMINATION OF AVERAGE VARIABLE COST
PER CENT FOR A HYPOTHETICAL PRODUCT MIX

Product	Variable Cost %	% of Total Sales	Cross-Product
A	60	20	0.120
B	65	20	0.130
C	70	20	0.140
D	75	30	0.225
E	80	10	0.080
Sum	—	100	0.695

The break-even volume for a particular mix of these products will lie on the break-even zone formed by the lower curve in Exhibit I at a point depending upon the average variable cost per cent (V) for the product mix. The average variable cost per cent for the product mix is determined (see table, Exhibit II) by weighting the variable cost per cent for each product by its percentage of total sales dollars, adding the cross-products, and substituting their sum for V in the general break-even equation.

The average variable cost per cent (V) for this product mix is 69.5%. The break-even volume (point M in Exhibit I) would be around $328,000:

$$\frac{\$100,000}{1 - 0.695} = \$327,869$$

This is the ordinate on the vertical axis of Exhibit I that corresponds with the abscissa variable cost per cent of 69.5 on the horizontal axis.

A profit curve can be added to enhance the analysis in Exhibit I. This curve represents the total sales required to obtain a specified profit margin. Add the desired profit per cent to each variable cost per cent, and substitute in the general break-even equation to calculate the points through which the profit curve (the upper curve in Exhibit I) will pass. For example, assuming a desired 10% profit margin, point A' is calculated as follows:

$$\frac{\$100,000}{1 - (0.60 + 0.10)} = \$333,333$$

The upper curve in Exhibit I shows the sales required to make a 10% net profit (before taxes) at each average variable cost per cent level for all possible combinations of the five products. Assuming the same product mix in Exhibit II, sales would have to be approximately $488,000:

$$\frac{\$100,000}{1 - (0.695 + 0.10)} = \$487,805$$

to make a 10% net profit. This point is M' on Exhibit I, the sales volume on the profit curve corresponding to an average variable cost per cent of 69.5.

SELLING PRICE VARIATIONS

Business analysts often must determine the effect of price changes on volume-cost-profit relationships. Locating the price and output at which profit would be maximized under a given set of circumstances is one of the main problems of traditional microeconomic analysis. Break-even analysis can be used for both these calculations if the basic break-even model is modified to include variations in selling price. The following example illustrates the method.

The variable cost per cent (V) and hence the break-even volume (S) decrease as the unit sales price increases. For example, if the unit variable cost is 60 cents and the unit sales price is one dollar, the variable cost per cent is 60 (or $0.60 divided by $1.00), while if the unit sales price were 90 cents with a unit variable cost of 60 cents, the variable cost per cent would be 67 ($0.60 over $0.90).

The curve in Exhibit III indicates how the break-even volume changes as the unit sales price is varied between 75 cents and one dollar, given total fixed costs of $100,000 and a variable unit cost of 60 cents.

To derive a function depicting the relationship between selling price and break-even volume, select, say, five different units sales prices, calculate the variable cost per cents, and substitute in the general break-even equation to obtain the break-even volume at each selling price. The break-even volume curve connecting these

EXHIBIT III

RELATION OF BREAK-EVEN VOLUME TO
SELLING PRICE

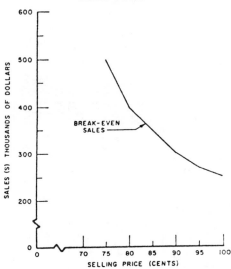

points (as in Exhibit III) will always be a rectangular hyperbola because of the nature of the general break-even function ($y = k/x$).

Exhibit V shows how to determine by break-even analysis the price and output at which profit would be maximized. Using the data in Exhibit IV, subtract "Break-Even Volume" (col. 6) from "Total Revenue," (col. 3) and from "Total Costs" (col. 4), and put the remainders in columns 7 and 8 respectively. Then plot these data from columns 7 and 8 (as is done in Exhibit V) in terms of the corresponding "Unit Sales Price" (col. 1 of Exhibit IV). Profit will be maximized at that price (and corresponding unit sales, or output, volume) where the spread between the curves is greatest. By inspection of Exhibit V (verified by columns 5 and 9 of Exhibit IV), the selling price that will maximize profit is approximately 95 cents, which corresponds to an anticipated sales (hence output) volume of 500,000 units in Exhibit IV. Note that the spread between the two curves in Exhibit V does *not* show dollars of profit, but merely the relative magnitude of profits at different selling prices.

EXHIBIT IV

HYPOTHETICAL DATA INVOLVED IN DETERMINING, BY BREAK-EVEN ANALYSIS, THE PRICE
AND OUTPUT AT WHICH PROFIT WOULD BE MAXIMIZED

Unit Sales Price (1)	Anticipated Unit Sales (2)	Total Revenue (3)	Total Costs (4)	Profit (5)	Break-Even Volume (6)	Total Revenue minus Break-Even Volume (7)	Total Costs minus Break-Even Volume (8)	Difference (Col. 7 minus Col. 8) (9)
$0.75	700,000	$525,000	$520,000	5,000	$500,000	$ 25,000	$ 20,000	$ 5,000
0.80	650,000	520,000	490,000	30,000	400,000	120,000	90,000	30,000
0.90	575,000	517,500	445,000	72,500	300,000	217,500	145,000	72,500
0.95	500,000	475,000	400,000	75,000	270,000	205,000	130,000	75,000
1.00	400,000	400,000	340,000	60,000	250,000	150,000	90,000	60,000

EXHIBIT V

APPLICATION OF BREAK-EVEN ANALYSIS TO
PRICE-OUTPUT DECISIONS

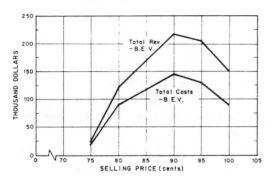

EXHIBIT VI

APPLICATION OF BREAK-EVEN ANALYSIS TO MECHANIZATION DECISIONS

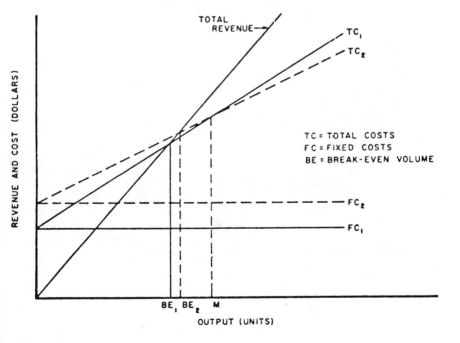

MECHANIZATION DECISIONS

Mechanization decisions arise with increasing frequency in the current era of automation. The basic break-even model also can be adapted to their solution. For example, if further mechanization would increase fixed costs by $200,000 and reduce variable costs by 30%, would it be wise to mechanize? Exhibit VI shows the application of break-even analysis in solving this problem. The solid lines represent the existing situation before mechanization, and the dashed lines represent the relationships that would result from mechanization.

Mechanization would obviously be unprofitable if forecasted sales were less than the new break-even volume (BE_2). At outputs between BE_2 and M the company would not lose money by mechanizing, but it would not make as much profit as before mechanization. The company definitely should mechanize if forecasted sales are greater than M, for it would then clear a larger unit profit than under the old production function.

0541154

5

Cost Accounting

Although evidences of the practice of cost accounting exist as far back as the Medieval period, it is, both with respect to problems encountered and concepts employed, essentially a product of the twentieth century.

The years between 1880 and 1920 represent a period of tremendous ferment in this area. Traditional accounting processes had failed to meet the needs of the post-Industrial Revolution era in providing information concerning the manufacturing costs of products and departments. An enthusiastic and expanding group of people with backgrounds in engineering and factory record keeping attempted to fill the void. For a time, widespread experimentation with cost systems occurred, but with the acceptance and integration of the cost accounts into the general and financial accounting structure around 1910, systems became more standardized in scope, and cost accounting took on an appearance within the accounts quite similar to its format in present-day cost systems.

In its beginnings cost accounting represented simply a procedure by which prime costs of manufacture were traced to products or processes. What to do with the newer costs associated with power-driven machinery represented an enigma. These costs, called *factory indirect expenses, manufacturing expenses,* or *manufacturing overhead,* gradually took on a position of significance in the triumvirate of manufacturing costs. A solution to the handling of these costs was found with the introduction of *overhead rates.* By means of these, a way was found to relate a vague body of manufacturing costs to a diverse group of products undergoing manufacture. Bases such as direct labor hours or machine hours were substituted for output as expressed by a variety of different product units.

Dividing manufacturing overhead cost by a common denominator of output made it possible to state the manufacturing overhead costs of individual products. This device, at first applied casually at year-end, evolved later into a careful and objective computation of overhead rates made before operations began, based upon expected production and forecasted costs. It made possible the costing of products for manufacturing overhead as operations progressed. This completed an orderly procedure by which all manufacturing costs are currently traced to products contained in inventory, and subsequently to cost of goods sold.

Formal Definition. Since cost accounting has been in a period of continuing development, any general definition attempting to present its meaning in a few words will tend to be incomplete, depending upon the particular interest of the user.

In its modern application, cost accounting may be defined as a phase of management controls integrated in part with the general financial records, which attempts to provide management with the cost of a variety of objects of interest, such as product, service, operation, area, plan, problem, or decision. In its initial impetus at the beginning of this century, as has been observed, cost accounting stressed the ascertainment of aggregate costs of manufacturing a product or rendering a service in a form suitable for incorporation into financial statements. Techniques for achieving this, particularly in the more complex areas of general overhead, material overhead, and labor overhead were well developed by 1945; and certain aspects of these were developed considerably earlier.

More recently, as indicated below, in the discussion of *Managerial Decision Making*, emphasis in cost accounting has shifted to encompass a wide variety of approaches to cost control, and to provide for a wide range of special data required for the solution of managerial decision-making problems. Consequently, differences between the terms *cost accounting* and *managerial accounting* have become blurred, and the terms are coming to be used interchangeably. (See Chapter 1, MANAGEMENT ACCOUNTING.)

STANDARD COST ACCOUNTING

Standard cost accounting with its emphasis upon "should be" costs determined prior to the incurrence of actual costs, was partly an outgrowth of the use of standards in connection with factory machines and operations, and partly an expansion of the concept of overhead rates into materials and labor accounting. Although ideas concerning standard costing had been advanced earlier, standard costs for manufacturing did not reach relative maturity until the decade beginning in 1930. In standard manufacturing accounting, a comparison is made between actual and standard costs by elements of expense for both products and departments. This is done with a view towards analyzing differences into controllable and noncontrollable causes and directing management's control efforts toward departments most needful of correction. (See Chapter 6, STANDARD COSTING.)

MARKETING COSTS

Cost accounting for marketing operations in contrast to manufacturing made little headway within formal accounting routines, and has over the years remained much in the process of development and experimentation. The subject received little consideration from accountants during the first forty years of this century, and such costing in the accounts proper has often been simply a matter of classifying expense items relating to distribution activities, either under one general marketing classification or under several sub-classifications such as warehousing, delivery, and sales promotion costs. Although recommendations in the right direction have been made sporadically since the 1930s, only relatively recently have accountants generally recognized the usefulness of flexible budgeting and standard costs to problems of marketing cost control and cost allocation. Today it is possible to compare within the accounts the actual and standard marketing costs of a variety of functions, to trace some of the distribution costs to products, and finally to obtain a knowledge of the standard marketing costs of various objects of managerial interest, such as a function, district, channel of trade, and class of customer. (See Chapter 13, MARKETING COST ANALYSIS.)

EXPANDED APPLICATIONS

Standard costing as it developed from 1920 to 1940 accustomed the accountant to deal with a variety of costs on a statistical basis, rather than upon the basis of costs recorded in the accounts according to generally accepted principles of accounting. Because standard costing requires a detailed analysis of costs and objective studies concerning their behavior, it laid the groundwork for the expansion in usefulness of cost accounting. This is evidenced by the development of direct costing and the application of cost analyses to the managerial decision-making area in recent decades.

The subject of fixed-variable cost analysis had received only isolated consideration at the beginning of this century. So had the concept of the break-even chart. (See Chapter 4, BREAK-EVEN ANALYSIS.) An analysis of costs into their fixed and variable elements is essential to the construction of overhead rates and an adequate accounting for overhead cost. As interest in volume-variation studies intensified during the 1940s, accountants took a more sophisticated view towards the fixed-variable cost classification. Statistical and mathematical techniques of least squares analysis and interpolation came into use to determine the reaction of costs to changes in operational activity. This made possible the categorization of an organization's or a department's costs into a formula which identified fixed and variable costs applicable to a range of output levels. Both direct costing and flexible budgeting rest upon this distinction.

Not only did the accountant arrive at a more precise means of analyzing costs into their fixed and variable elements, but he came to a mature understanding of fixed costs. He came to understand that the term "fixed costs" has validity only in the short run; most costs are variable over the long run. A number of costs classified as fixed are actually discretionary in nature, for example, costs of frequent repainting or certain types of grounds maintenance. Finally, in recent decades, the accountant recognized that the particular composition of fixed costs has relevance only to the problem posed. Annual costs of space may be pertinent to the problem of ascertaining costs for profit determination purposes; however, its cost (at least in the current year) may be irrelevant to the problem of utilizing such space.

VARIABLE COSTING

By 1950, the idea of "direct costing"—now more commonly referred to in the literature as "variable costing"—had gained prominence in accounting and management circles. Variable costing is partly a method of cost assignment applicable to financial accounting problems wherein manufacturing costs designated as "direct" (variable costs) are traced to specific items produced, and are therefore subdivided in the accounting process between inventories and cost of goods sold; also, variable selling and administrative expenses are separated from fixed selling and administrative expenses. Direct costing is also a method of analysis attempting to identify for a variety of managerial purposes those costs which vary by products, operations, departments, and branches. Focus of attention on variable costs is believed to provide a better basis of managerial control over the operation of areas of responsibility and also to provide management with a better basis for decisions in the short run concerning profitable products and departments. (See Chapter 11, DIRECT (VARIABLE) COSTING.)

THE COST ACCOUNTING STANDARDS BOARD

The Cost Accounting Standards Board (CASB) is a creature of the Congress of the United States (1970), established to "promulgate cost accounting standards designed to achieve uniformity and consistency in the cost accounting principles followed" under certain cost-basis, negotiated Federal contracts. The Board consists of five members including the Comptroller General of the United States and four of his appointees. Of the latter, two are chosen from the accounting profession, one from industry, and a fourth from some branch of the Federal Government. The CASB is assisted by a prescribed staff of 25 professional members.

Initially, the standards of the Board applied to defense contracts of $100,000 and over. By 1975, standards of the Board had been extended to all negotiated Federal contracts, defense and non-defense, where the initial contract amounted to $500,000 or more.

To date, the Board has promulgated the following standards:[1]

401 Consistency in estimating, accumulating and reporting costs.
402 Consistency in allocating costs incurred for the same purpose.
403 Allocation of home office expense to segments.
404 Capitalization of tangible assets.
405 Accounting for unallowed costs.
406 Cost accounting period.
407 Use of standard costs for direct material and direct labor.
408 Accounting for costs of compensated personal absence.
409 Depreciation of tangible capital assets.
410 Allocation of general and administrative expenses.
411 Accounting for acquisition costs of materials.
412 Composition and measurement of pension costs.
413 (Withdrawn) Adjustment of historical depreciation costs for inflation.
414 Cost of money as an element of the cost of capital.
415 Deferred compensation costs.

A significant aspect of the CASB's work is its promulgation of Disclosure Statement regulations. Certain contractors subject to the Board must complete statements which bring to light whether or not they are consistently following practices certified by the Board. These statements also provide information helpful to the Board in studying the need for new standards.

MANAGERIAL DECISION MAKING

Although the results of the first 50 years' effort in cost accounting in this century are apparent in modern cost finding and control systems, the dynamic area of cost accountancy today lies in an opportunity and incremental approach toward determining costs essential to a variety of managerial decisions. Relative to the problem of expansion or contraction of operations, for example, only variable and incremental fixed costs may be considered. With

---

[1] Interested readers can obtain explanatory rulings in full, concerning standards promulgated and their effective dates, from The Cost Accounting Standards Board, 441 G Street N.W., Washington, D.C. 20548.

regard to the decision on whether to drop a product, a host of opportunity and incremental revenue and cost factors will be studied, such as revenues lost and costs avoided by the discontinuance, and effects upon sales and profit contributions of other products. Capital budgeting studies pose the "opportunity costs" of one investment possibility as contrasted to an alternative one. An infinite variety of cost concepts such as incremental, variable, sunk, replacement, discretionary, and imputed costs will be used as contrasted to the application of aggregate historical costs when costing manufacturing inventories.

Not only does modern cost accounting array and analyze costs on an individual basis with respect to products, branches, or alternative investments, it also supplies cost data relevant to overall planning, scheduling, and control of projects involving numerous complex and alternative operations.

6
Standard Costing

Standard costing refers to the establishment of cost standards and their application to problems of management, particularly those problems relating to product costs and departmental cost control.

Standard costs consist of allowed amounts of various cost factors, such as: materials, direct labor, manufacturing overhead, marketing, and administrative cost, as well as subdivisions of these, expressed in a variety of terms such as: pounds, tons, hours, invoice lines, and salesman's calls, all weighted by dollars. Although the overwhelming practice is to apply these standards in the course of operations, daily, weekly, and monthly, standards are sometimes established and applied at the conclusion of relatively long periods of operations, for example, a year.

There are three distinguishing characteristics of standard costs: (1) they are based upon objective experimentation or a careful study of past experience, or upon a combination of both procedures; (2) the nature, quality, and makeup of a product in terms of materials, labor, and facility requirements are carefully established; and (3) the productive or functional processes through which the product moves are carefully studied for integration and standardization.

USES OF STANDARD COST

Standard costs:

(1) Provide a basis against which actual costs may be compared, and deviations from standards expressed in quantitative terms for

ready use in the evaluation of efficiency at some level of an organization's operations.

(2) Provide for the assignment of costs representative of the actual costs on a consistent basis to production inventories and cost of goods sold.

(3) Expedite the ascertainment of profits during the interim on a product, departmental, or plant level.

(4) Are utilized in the preparation of budgets and in planning.

(5) Are useful as a guide to pricing present and prospective products or services.

(6) Provide data useful to a study of alternatives, particularly where the problem calls for a knowledge of activity costs by specified operations.

(7) Add to convenience in accounting routine, particularly in connection with raw materials, work in process, and finished goods accounting.

Considerable controversy raged in the late 1920s and during the 1930s concerning the proper interpretation of standard costs of manufacturing: Should they be considered simply as units of measure to be employed entirely on a statistical basis outside the accounts proper, or as having a value representative of actual costs and capable of recording in the accounts?

By and large, the latter interpretation won out, and most accountants interpret standard manufacturing costs as costs representative of actual costs ideally suited to measure the flow of manufacturing costs through work in process, finished goods, and cost of goods sold accounts. For a great many purposes, greater reliance will be placed upon these figures during the course of a fiscal period than upon the accumulating historical cost data. For example, in the interim, standard costs take precedence over the recorded historical costs for most reporting purposes. A similar concensus concerning the integration of standard marketing costs into the formal accounts has not taken place, largely because it is generally assumed that most marketing costs are not applicable to product units. In contrast to practice with respect to standard manufacturing costs, standard marketing costs are widely used both on an independent statistical basis as well as on an integrated account basis.

CONCEPTS

Standard costs may be established upon the basis of: (1) the best or average costs incurred in the past; (2) what costs are expected to be for the period under consideration under ordinary conditions of control; (3) the level of costs attainable under optimum conditions of control but not necessarily ideal with respect to efficiency of workers and equipment; and (4) what costs would be under ideal conditions of control and efficiency.

Standard costs of the nature of (1), above, should be used with considerable caution. The best costs of the past may have been entirely accidental in nature and not attainable in the future, or represent extremely poor performance relative to what is possible under good conditions of control. Similarly, an average of past costs represents a mixture of both good and bad experience weighted by the contingencies under which they took place. In general, because the very objective of standard costing is to improve upon past performance, standard costs based entirely upon past experience neither provide an incentive for improvement, nor are representative of the actual costs if the desired improvements take place.

Standard costs commonly referred to as "current" tend to partake of concepts indicated in points (2) and (3). When standard costs are established on the basis of what costs are expected to be under ordinary conditions of control, point (2), they tend to be attainable in nature and quite representative of accumulating actual costs. In the construction of such standards, allowance is made for the fact that it is difficult to maintain maximum efficiency continuously over extended periods of time. Sizable variances arising when such standards are employed indicate serious deviations from anticipated costs.

When standards are established on the basis of the level of costs attainable under optimum conditions of control, point (3), they become less attainable on a day-to-day basis. Such standards may be achieved sporadically over short periods of time, particularly toward the close of an operating period after considerable experience has been had in attempting to meet them. Although these higher but attainable standards provide more of a stimulus to cost reduction than standards of the order of (2), above, they will be less representative of accumulating actual costs. Because of this, sizable variances may be less serious in nature than variances arising in connection with the expected cost type of standard. When best attainable standards are used, variances will tend to be the rule rather than the exception.

Ideal standards, point (4), signify standards not currently attainable with present facilities and personnel. Although students of modern behavioral psychology point on occasion to situations where some people perform more efficiently when a goal is placed beyond their attainment, the concensus is that standards of the ideal type frustrate rather than stimulate improvement. Consequently, such standards are ordinarily useless for day-to-day performance control purposes. Because ideal standard costs are hypothetical, they have no place in the inventory and cost-of-goods-sold accounts. Their use would give rise continuously to significant variances. Ideal standard costs, however, are pertinent to certain comparisons made on a statistical basis. For example, the differences in cost obtained when these standards are applied to output as contrasted to an application of current standard costs provide an excellent measurement of the opportunity costs of not utilizing the most efficient equipment and personnel.

CURRENT COST STANDARDS

When standard costs are computed on a current basis, the immediate future for the most part becomes the concern of the accountant. Forecasts of material prices, for example, may be used to determine material price standards; labor rates will emanate from union contracts or rates expected to prevail. Similarly, with respect to the price aspect of other costs factors, reference will be made to circumstances expected in the forthcoming fiscal period.

The establishment of usage standards varies, depending upon the "tightness" of standards contemplated. Where standards tending toward the ideal are utilized, physical quantities indicated by engineering drawings, weighing, or measuring of a model of the product to be produced, provide the basis for the usage aspect of the material cost standard. Similarly, time and motion studies may

EXHIBIT I
STANDARD PRODUCT COST CARD

STANDARD PRODUCT COST CARD

Product Name————————————   Product Code No.————————

Material Costs

Code No.	Quantity Allowed Per Unit	Price Per Lb./Item	Total Cost Per Unit	Total Cost Per Unit
B–225X	1/2	$0.50	$0.25	
L–217	2	1.00	2.00	
W–257	1	.20	.20	
		Total Material Cost Per Unit		$2.45

Direct Labor Costs

Dept. and Op. No.	D.L. Hrs. Allowed Per Unit	Labor Rates	Total Cost Per Unit	
105	.10	$4.00	$0.40	
107	.20	4.00	.80	
210	.50	3.00	1.50	
		Total Direct Labor Cost Per Unit		2.70

Manufacturing Overhead Costs

Dept. and Op. No.	D.L. Hrs. Allowed Per Unit	Overhead Rates	Total Cost Per Unit	
105	.10	$3.00	$0.30	
107	.20	3.00	.60	
210	.50	2.00	1.00	
		Total Manufacturing Overhead Cost Per Unit		1.90
		TOTAL STANDARD COST PER UNIT		$7.05

be employed to establish labor usage studies. At the other extreme, past experience may be brought to bear to allow for expected over-use of materials and labor time. In between these two divergent concepts of tightness or looseness, a range of attainable standards is employed in the construction of current cost standards calling for varying exertion upon the part of management and employees to reach standards established.

STANDARD PRODUCT COST CARD

Although a variety of business forms may be utilized in connection with standard costing, the standard product cost card or sheet is basic to the operation of a standard cost system on either a statistical or integrated account basis. The standard product cost card first shows physical quantities of materials allowed per unit of a particular product with quantities extended at standard prices. Subsequent sections of the card display in similar detail standard labor and overhead costs, as shown in Exhibit I.

All of the data shown on the standard product cost card will be supported by a great variety of complementary business forms, in which productive activity may be broken down by operations, and supervisory responsibility subdivided by cost centers. Thus, in addition to the standard product card illustrated, there may be:

An *operational standard cost sheet* detailing the variable standard costs of an operation.

A *cost center standard fixed cost sheet* showing all the fixed costs of a center on a flexible budget basis and including a computation of the center's normal overhead rate.

A *cost center control form* used to display actual and standard costs deemed controllable by the cost center supervisor.

SETTING STANDARD COSTS

Materials.   Standard material prices are best established upon the basis of budgeting and forecasting, where possible looking forward to actual contracts for materials placed. When this is done, the material price standard for a particular item of material may be obtained by (1) adding together costs of anticipated purchases of the item and the current standard cost of the expected opening inventory, and (2) dividing the total cost of the two by the number of units involved. Alternatively, current invoice prices or vendor price lists adjusted for anticipated movements in prices may be relied upon as a basis for the material price standard.

Standard material quantities are best determined by reference to engineering drawings, weighing, measuring, and calculating, or by using experience gleaned from test runs. Standard allowances for waste or spoilage are similarly computed, and their sale value is used to diminish gross standard material cost. Alternatively, standard material usage may be based upon a careful analysis and study of past experience concerning material usage.

Labor. Standard labor rates are established by reference to union contracts or prevailing rates of pay, taking into consideration their possible incorporation into wage incentive plans. For purposes of standard costing, the labor rate is best established by setting rates by tasks to be accomplished rather than on an individual employee basis. With regard to a particular department or operational area, the labor rate is often computed by taking a total of standard payments made for a variety of tasks in an area and dividing this total by the standard hours of work.

Standard labor allowances are computed on the basis of: (1) past experience, (2) simple observation, (3) time and motion studies, (4) predetermined motion times standards such as "motion time measurement" (MTM) where tables are available indicating the time values of various physical motions, and (5) generalizing and tying together random observations by means of statistical methods. Standard labor allowances per unit of product priced at standard labor rates are shown by departments on the standard product cost card in Exhibit I.

Manufacturing Overhead. Standard overhead rates are established by a computation which divides the standard budgeted overhead costs of an area by an appropriate quantitative expression of operating activity. Keeping in mind the relationship between materiality and the cost and convenience of accounting, the most useful expression of the overhead costs of an area on an activity unit basis results from basing the rate on the costs of a carefully delimited single operational area or on the costs of a related group of operations. Conversely, the larger area for which overhead rates are constructed, the less validity do the resulting unit costs have to problems of costing a variety of products undergoing divergent processing.

A center of controversy in standard manufacturing accounting since 1920 has been the appropriate concept of the denominator of the standard fixed cost overhead formula: whether it should express maximum potential use of facilities, average use, or some attainable level of capacity. The term "normal overhead" is often applied to such concepts of the denominator of the standard overhead rate formula. Standard rates based on average use of capacity or an attainable level of capacity tend to channel fixed overhead costs which approximate actual fixed costs to products produced over a series of years. Where a maximum capacity measurement of the denominator of the overhead formula is employed, fixed costs attached to products during protracted periods of idleness become less representative of the actual fixed costs taking place. However, the resulting idle capacity variance provides a rather absolute measure of inability to operate at maximum capacity.

The denominator of the manufacturing overhead formula is customarily measured by such activity bases as: direct labor hours, direct labor cost, machine hours, and prime cost. Needless to say, such bases ought to be representative of the activity of the area to which they are applied. It may be noted that in automated industries, labor hours or labor cost have in fact become auxiliary to the operation of machinery. Rather than use a labor basis of overhead allocation, it can be argued that use of a machine hour basis and the inclusion of labor cost of tenders in the numerator of the overhead formula would result in a more useful method of tracing costs to product.

Once a quantity expressive of the normal level of output has been established, the standard overhead rate may be computed by dividing budgeted overhead costs of an area by this quantity. For example, referring to Dept. No. 16, Exhibit II, if normal output were defined as 70,000 direct labor hours, the normal overhead

EXHIBIT II
FLEXIBLE BUDGET SHOWING COST BY LEVELS OF OUTPUT
Department No. 16

Expense	Direct Labor Hours					
	40,000	50,000	60,000	70,000	80,000	90,000
Indirect Materials	$1,000	$1,250	$1,500	$ 1,750	$ 2,000	$ 2,250
Power	400	500	600	700	800	900
Indirect Labor	1,800	2,200	2,600	3,000	3,400	3,800
Maintenance	300	350	400	450	500	550
Supplies	550	650	750	850	950	1,050
Miscellaneous	950	1,100	1,250	1,400	1,550	1,700
Depreciation	500	500	500	500	500	500
Space Occupancy	400	400	400	400	400	400
Supervision	1,000	1,000	1,000	1,000	1,000	1,000
Totals	$6,900	$7,950	$9,000	$10,050	$11,100	$12,150

rate for the area would be established as follows:

Budgeted Overhead Cost at 70,000 DLH
——————————————————————————
            Normal Capacity in DLH

$$= \frac{\$10,050}{70,000} = \$0.1435 \text{ per DLH}$$

Alternatively, referring to the data given in Exhibit III, the rate for Dept. No. 16 may be subdivided into a fixed and variable rate and expressed as follows:

$$\frac{\text{Budgeted Fixed Overhead Cost}}{\text{Normal Capacity in DLH}} = \frac{\$2,700}{70,000} = \$0.0385$$

Fixed Overhead Rate per DLH = $0.0385
Variable Overhead Rate per DLH (from Exhibit III) = <u>0.1050</u>
Total Overhead Rate per DLH = 0.1435

EXHIBIT III
FLEXIBLE BUDGET SHOWING COSTS BY FIXED
AND VARIABLE ELEMENTS
Department No. 16

	Fixed Amount (if any)	Variable Rate
Indirect Materials		$0.025
Power		.010
Indirect Labor	$ 200	.040
Maintenance	100	.005
Supplies	150	.010
Miscellaneous	350	.015
Depreciation	500	
Space Occupancy	400	
Supervision	1,000	
	$2,700	$0.105

STANDARD COST VARIANCES DEFINED

Variances in standard costing refer to differences between actual and standard costs for specified areas of operational activity and are usually expressed in dollars. Brief descriptions of common variances follow.

Material Price Variance. Difference between actual and standard material costs because actual material prices differ from standard material prices.

Material Usage Variance. Difference between actual and standard material cost because actual quantities consumed differ from standard quantities allowed.

Labor Rate Variance. Difference between actual and standard labor cost, because actual labor rate differs from standard labor rate.

Labor Usage Variance. Difference between actual and standard labor cost because actual labor hours employed to produce the output differ from the standard labor hours allowed for that output.

Overhead Capacity Variance. Difference between actual and standard overhead costs due ordinarily to the fact that operating activity (hours facilities were used) has been above or below normal activity on which standards were based. The measure of operating activity may be standard time allowed for good product achieved under the "2-variance method" or actual time operated under the "3-variance method." (Refer to foregoing discussion, "Setting Standard Costs: Manufacturing Overhead"; see also Section on FLEXIBLE BUDGETING in Chapter 10, BUDGETING.)

Overhead Budget Variance. Under the 3-variance method, the difference between actual and standard overhead cost because of above- or below-standard efficiency relative to expense incurrence. Under the 2-variance method, this variance is also expressive of the standard variable cost of time misused. (See Section on FLEXIBLE BUDGETING in Chapter 10, BUDGETING.)

Overhead Efficiency Variance. Difference between actual and standard overhead cost due to above- or below-standard efficiency in the time required to produce the output.

COMPUTATION OF VARIANCES

A difference between actual and standard costs may be subdivided in innumerable ways preparatory to further analysis into the cause of the variance. For example, the fact that $5,100 was spent for 1,200 hours of labor when a standard $4,000 should have been spent for 1,000 hours may be explained as indicated in Exhibit IV.

Exhibit IV
Computation of Variances

Labor Usage Variance, 200 additional hours taken at the $4.00 standard hourly rate	$ 800	Labor Usage Variance
Labor Rate Variance, 1,200 hours of labor paid for at 25¢ per hour in excess of the standard hourly rate	300	Labor Rate Variance
Total Labor Variance	$1,100	

Alternatively, the $1,100 variance may be subdivided into:

Payment for delays while waiting for work, 100 delay hours at $4.00 standard rate	$ 400	Labor Delay Variance
Inefficient use of 100 hours of labor	400	Labor Usage Variance
Money paid because of failure to earn $3.00 an hour guaranteed	240	Make-Up Money Variance
Payment of 5¢ an hour in excess of standard labor rate	60	Labor Rate Variance
	$1,100	

EXHIBIT V
COMPUTATION OF MANUFACTURING OVERHEAD VARIANCE
(2-Variance Method)

	(1) Standard Quantity at Std. Prices or Rates	(2) Actual Quantity at Std. Prices or Rates	(3) Actual Quantity at Actual Pr. or Rate	(4) Total (1) − (3)	(5) Variance Usage (1) − (2)	(6) Pr. or Rate (2) − (3)
Materials:	$2 \times 700 \times \$1 = \$1,400$	$1500 \times \$1 = \$1,500$	$1500 \times \$1.10 = \$1,650$	$250	$100	$150
Labor:	$1 \times 700 \times \$4 = \$2,800$	$800 \times \$4 = \$3,200$	$800 \times \$4.10 = \$3,280$	$480	$400	$ 80

SOURCE: Adapted from Schiff and Benninger, "Cost Accounting."

EXHIBIT VI
COMPUTATION OF MANUFACTURING OVERHEAD VARIANCE
(3-Variance Method)

(1) Hours Allowed at Std. Rate	(2) Budget Allowed For Std. Hours in Product	(3) Budget Allowed For Actual Hrs. Worked	(4) Actual Overhead	(5) Total (1) − (4)	(6) Capacity (1) − (2)	(7) Efficiency (2) − (3)	(8) Budget (3) − (4)
700 × $6	(700) Fixed $2000 Var. 2800	(800) Fixed $2000 Var. 3200					
$4200	$4800	$5200	$5300	$1100	$600	$400	$100

SOURCE: Adapted from Schiff and Benninger, "Cost Accounting."

Keeping the foregoing in mind, a conventional computation of variances is shown in Exhibits V and VI.

Common methods of constructing variances have been criticized unfavorably from time to time on the following scores:

(1) They lump together in one or more figures differences between actual and standard costs, some of which may be controllable at the operating level for which drawn, some of which may not. (See Section on FLEXIBLE BUDGETING in Chapter 10, BUDGETING.)

(2) They represent in one amount so many causes of variances that further analysis is necessary. For example, a material usage variance may be due to: inferior materials, excessive application of materials (paint), excessive scrap, loss of materials because of machine breakdown, and spoilage of product containing materials. Also, all the cost of excess usage may not be included in the material usage variance amount (see next item).

(3) The content of variances which are isolated are not mutually exclusive. Excess material usage may aggravate a materials price variance by calling for a greater consumption of materials at above standard prices. A portion of the material price variance may therefore be caused by excess material consumption. A similar problem exists with labor and overhead variances, in the case of the latter particularly in connection with the 2-variance method of overhead analysis.

DISPOSITION OF VARIANCES

When a standard cost system is utilized, variances may be occasioned by:

(1) Errors in the construction of standards.

(2) Inefficiency of expenditure or in the use of labor time and facilities.

(3) Purposely setting standards beyond what is currently attainable as a stimulus to increased productivity.

(4) Failure to utilize capacity as anticipated in the computation of the normal overhead rate.

(1) Errors in the construction of standards may represent simply a mistake in estimating price, rates, or the attainable level

of performance. The necessary information was available at the time standards were established. Had standards been properly computed, they would have been valid throughout the period in question. Variances in this instance are the responsibility of the standard setter. On the other hand, errors may be due to a change in circumstances: higher prices occasioned by shortages brought on by a war or below-standard performance resulting from unexpected orders and the necessity of hiring relatively unskilled labor. In this latter case, it is assumed that the change, under the circumstances, could not have been known at the time standards were established, and, consequently, no one in the organization may be held responsible for ensuing variances. Regardless of whether the error giving rise to variances was due to a mistake in judgment or to changing conditions, if the error is significant in amount, and if feasible, accounts misstated because of the error need to be modified by the amount of the variance or variances. If the variance is nominal in amount, it is closed out as a periodic item.

(2) If there is excess expenditure or if labor time and facilities have been misused, variances should be tied to their cause: defective materials, machine break-downs, unnecessary delays, or simply shoddy performance. They should then be brought to the attention of the supervisor responsible. Where there is *under-absorbed* fixed overhead cost due to the fact that overhead rates have been premised on good production attainable and such production has not been attained because of inefficiency, the variance again should be charged to the supervisor responsible. Some authorities hold that variances due to inefficiency are losses, not costs, and favor their showing as period deductions on the income statement. Others argue that, in any event, these variances represent additional costs and should therefore be prorated as applicable to inventories and cost of goods sold. Again, if the variance is insignificant in amount, it is summarily disposed of to profit and loss.

(3) When standards are purposely set higher than is attainable on a continuous basis, resulting variances become a mixture of "losses" and figures representing the cost of inability to achieve presently unattainable goals. If the attainable level of performance is known, variances due to inefficiency should be separated out and treated as in (2), above. The portion of such variances which

measure the opportunity cost of utilizing present personnel and facilities is disposed of, following proper reporting to planning administration, much like variances in (1), above.

(4) Where fixed overhead costs remain under- or overabsorbed because of anticipated fluctuations in the use of facilities, theoretically the variance, debit or credit, should be deferred. However, it is common to allocate such variances when significant to inventories and cost of goods sold; otherwise to dispose of them simply as a period deduction.

STANDARD COSTING APPLIED TO MARKETING ACTIVITIES

Standard manufacturing cost accounting stresses relating manufacturing costs to products and departments and the importance of comparing actual and standard costs on these levels. From its very beginnings, marketing cost accounting has been less concerned with product costs, in part because of the tracing and allocation difficulties involved, and has instead attempted to effect other tracings and allocations useful to cost control and analyses of special interest to management. Standard marketing costing is employed to determine the marketing costs of a wide range of objects of managerial interest, such as: function, responsibility level, district operation, channel of trade, class of customer, salesman, and product.

In contrast to what is commonly found in manufacturing cost accounting, namely that direct costs often make up .a significant portion of total manufacturing cost, marketing costs capable of direct tracing to the ultimate object of interest, such as district, salesman, or channel of trade, may be quite small relative to the total of such costs. Consequently, an initial analysis attempting to subdivide marketing costs between those which are capable of direct tracing to the object or objects of interest and those which are not, ordinarily ends with a sizable group of unallocated costs.

In manufacturing cost accounting, costs termed "indirect" to product are commonly taken to departmental classifications prior to product application. Similarly, "indirect" marketing costs are customarily traced to functional classifications such as storing, packing and shipping, order processing and billing, and advertising.

Once such a tracing has been accomplished, the parallel between manufacturing cost accounting and marketing cost accounting tends to end, partly because the ensuing object of managerial interest in marketing cost accounting analysis may not be products, and partly because of the difficulties of relating a large body of marketing costs to products even through management may be interested in such an association. (See Chapter 13, MARKETING COST ANALYSIS.)

ESTIMATED vs. STANDARD COSTS

Sometimes an attempt is made to distinguish between standard costs and a related, term *estimated costs.* Cost estimates of varying degrees of accuracy and reliability may be employed intermittently as desired, outside the formal accounting structure. Where the estimates are incorporated in the accounts and the accounts themselves are made to show differences between actual and estimated costs, cost accounting of the estimated type may be said to exist. Used this way, estimated costs assigned to work in process and finished goods inventories are substituted for an analysis and allocation of currently incurred historical costs. An estimated cost system may be defined therefore as one in which estimated unit costs of a product are used to price inventories of work in process and finished goods shown in the ledger accounts.

An important advantage in the use of estimates within the formal accounting system is that burdensome detail and paper work inherent in a cost accounting system dealing entirely with actual costs is reduced or eliminated when an estimated cost system is employed. Work in process and finished goods control accounts as well as their supporting detail are kept in terms of estimates. Differences between estimated and actual costs are abstracted and isolated in variation accounts.

When estimated costs differ from actual costs, the usual assumption is that the estimates were incorrectly computed. This is in sharp contrast to the understanding which exists when a standard cost system is employed, where when variances arise it is generally assumed that the actual costs are wrong. Consequently, when it is ascertained periodically that actual costs differ from estimated costs, there is a strong impetus to correct estimated data contained in inventory and cost of goods sold accounts. However, since the strength of estimated cost systems rests upon their convenience, complex and precise procedures for the allocation of variations will ordinarily not be followed, and when tenable, the variance will be closed out to the income account as a period charge. Estimated costs serve only incidentally and then rather poorly as a medium for cost control. Where it is desired to secure variances expressing differences between actual and "should be" costs by *causes,* it is much more satisfactory to adopt a thoroughgoing standard cost system.

Probabilistic Standards. Much interest has been displayed in recent years concerning the use of probabilistic control standards either of the quality control type or of types which are more subjective in nature as suggested by modern decision theory. Advocates of the use of probabilistic models argue that considerable time and effort are spent in traditional standard costing, in investigating variances which, in fact, represent operations within the bounds of normal performance. Further, they argue that the cost of investigation in the traditional standard costing model often exceeds the savings achieved.

7
Cost Control

The term *Cost Control* as used in a larger and more general sense is applicable to all actions of management designed to accomplish objectives relative to the cost phase of profit maximization. In this context, then, cost control would embrace all activities designed to influence costs in planning and policy determination and cost applicable to all phases of operations management: research, production, marketing, and financial.

Cost accounting in this larger sense plays an active role in providing costs pertinent to contemplated policy moves, costs associated with plant expansion or contraction, and, at the operational level, providing cost data relative to special problems of management: inventory minimum order points, economic lot size, cost of auditing vendor invoices, costs of alternative wage incentive plans, cost of alternative capital investment decisions, and a host of other special problem and decision-requiring situations.

FORMAL DEFINITION

Even though all of the above activities expedite control in a very real and fundamental sense, the term cost control as employed in cost accounting does not ordinarily refer to the foregoing, and is used in a more restricted fashion. Cost control as commonly used in cost accounting might better be called "performance control." It has to do with securing compliance with a prescribed plan or policy.

APPROACHES AND TECHNIQUES

The term "cost control" is applied to a variety of techniques and procedures, including underlying concepts, employed by the accountant to assist management in achieving the cost phase of profit maximization at particular responsibility levels. Typically this methodology involves some form of cost comparison. Stress is placed on an analysis of cost by persons, provision of information concerning the manager's role relative to a plan or budget, and establishment of cost standards and the reporting of deviations thereof. Most writers on the subject present three phases of cost control: (1) comparison of present performance with predetermined standards; (2) taking corrective action if feasible; and (3) incorporation of the results of steps (1) and (2) into planning (utilization of cost feedback or cost "feedforward").

Use of departmental, process, or branch systems of cost accounting, particularly in connection with standard costs or budgets, epitomize the service of cost accounting in furthering managerial cost control. Such systems premise control guidance upon a comparison of historically accumulated costs of an area of supervision with past, budgeted, or standard costs. Differences between historically accumulated costs and the benchmark chosen are studied as a guide to remedial action. In both flexible budgeting and standard costing, such differences are intended to play a major and positive role in directing individual efforts toward minimizing costs. Managerial incentive pay systems are sometimes premised upon the achievement of standard costs and the elimination of unfavorable variances.

Similar techniques are applied to accounting for company divisions in an effort to assure efficient divisional performance and control. Not only is control attempted by means of comparisons of costs with standards and budgets, but costs are matched against divisional revenues to secure a divisional profit and loss figure. Measurement of divisional income may be used as a basis of control, or, instead, the computation of rate of return on divisional investment may be attempted.

Divisional rates of return may be compared, one division to the other, or the rate of return may be compared with a separately constructed benchmark for each division.

HUMAN RELATIONS STUDIES AND COST CONTROL

As a consequence of behavioristic studies in business, a subtle but significant change has taken place in the prevailing philosophy of cost control, especially since 1960. Although such thinking has affected the mechanics of cost control, particularly in the establishment of accounts which cover a more carefully defined and delimited area of managerial responsibility, its most cogent effect has been in the area of account data utilization.

Construction of budgetary and cost standards in the new milieu are thought of more as phases of planning and are developed where feasible with the cooperation of the supervisor of the area to which the standards apply. The ideal is to have the manager set his *own* goals within the framework of the broader company objectives, with the hope that he will develop a feeling of responsibility for achieving them. When budgets or standards are not achieved, the comparisons carry less the connotation of the odious and more of the need to study and explain changes which have affected their achievement. (See Section, RESPONSIBILITY REPORTING in Chapter 10, BUDGETING.) Thus the thrust of this approach is to substitute the more positive profit-generating goals and measures for the psychologically negative cost incentives and controls traditionally applied to production executives and supervisors.

8

Overhead Assignment

Overhead assignment is a two-way process. One is to charge an appropriate amount of general expense to the business done in a period of time. The other is to assign a correct amount of overhead to a part or a product so as to know its total cost. The simplest, though somewhat incorrect, illustration of the latter is the mark-up method used by stores in setting prices. The difference between mark-up and overhead assignment is the percentage included in mark-up for profit.

Overhead assignment is necessary because only two of three general types of costs in industry are directly related to products—*direct labor* and *direct material*. Direct labor and direct material are charged directly to specific parts and products. All other costs incurred are classified as indirect or overhead. These expenses must be assigned one way or another to the business carried on so as to obtain its total cost. The same is true when computing the cost of a part or a product.

Before the advent of systematic cost accounting, profit was "the money left over in the cash drawer." It was the difference between the money taken in and the amounts paid out. That method of reckoning is still used by many small enterprisers. But today much more precision is required in most companies for two principal reasons: One is that they turn out many more products, and need to know what the potential profit or loss is on *each one*. The other stems from requirements for public accounting to stockholders and for taxes.

The "cash-drawer method" is not precise enough because the time of accounting rarely coincides with actual receipts and payments. Often, the largest amount of overlap is in the dollars represented by inventory. Some of these dollars are in finished goods not sold, some are in work-in-process, and some are in materials purchased but not used. Some overhead is ruled to be part of the cost of finished goods and of work-in-process. These amounts of overhead can be very large in companies that build up stocks in off-seasons to prepare for anticipated demands. In a like manner, large amounts accrue when complex products require months of time to complete.

Other examples of items of actual overhead expense out of phase with accounting periods are advertising, taxes, and insurance. These are paid for when due, but are not wholly assignable to that period's costs. Still another is the controversial expense of depreciation or depletion. The argument is about the time interval over which the cost shall be spread.

In the accounting-period profit and loss statement, overhead assignment is commonly done in two parts. One is the direct assignment of actual sales expense and administrative expenses to the goods sold during the period. These expenses show as a deduction from gross profit. The other part is in the portion of cost of goods sold that is built up of manufacturing overheads already assigned to the products as they were being made. Thus, usually, overhead is separated into two major categories primarily because of the time interval between making and selling the products. One part of overhead is termed Sales and Administrative, the other Manufacturing, Overhead, or Burden.

Generally, these two overheads are assigned differently, as the foregoing indicates. Usually, the total actual expense of Sales and Administrative for the period is charged against the actual sales income for that period. In contrast, most of Manufacturing Overhead is charged *pro-rata* through cost of sales by means of portions assigned to parts and products.

MANUFACTURING OVERHEAD

Much of the attention to overhead assignment devolves upon computations of manufacturing overhead costs. This process was fairly simple in earlier times when the variety of products made was small. To illustrate with an oversimplication, when Henry Ford turned out only the Model T, he could get the overhead cost per car by simply dividing total overhead costs by total automobile production. Similarly shoe manufacturers computed overhead costs per dozen pairs. By reasoning that tons were finished products, steel mills and foundries assigned overhead costs by calculating overhead rates per ton. Textile mills computed overhead costs per yard.

The approaches used in the foregoing cases are methods of arriving at the objective of overhead costs per unit of product. But as companies developed more designs and acquired more products, they could no longer correctly use counts such as pieces, tons, yards or dozens as divisors. It became necessary to devise another method for assigning overhead. The newer method was based on choosing a common denominator that could be used to add together unlike products.

As a common denominator, many metal fabricators chose *machine hours*. Most companies selected *direct labor*. Some used both by assigning certain overheads to machine hours and others to direct labor. The term direct labor as used here includes four different denominators—*dollars* of labor, *actual* or *measured*; and *hours* of labor, *actual* or *measured.*

This procedure involves an intermediate step, namely to compute an *overhead rate* per unit of time or labor dollar. Then this rate is used to assign the overhead cost to the product made and sold. This common procedure consists of three basic steps:

(1) Determine amounts of production volume and overhead expenses that correspond.

(2) Divide expenses by volumes to obtain overhead rates.

(3) Multiply an overhead rate by the specific volume involved in a particular operation, part, assembly, or period to compute the overhead assigned.

Because Step 2 results in one or more overhead cost rates, there are many different approaches made in Step 1. The basic one goes back to the beginning of this discussion. It has to do with sorting *direct* from *indirect* labor. Whatever is called direct labor goes in the denominator (divisor) in Step 2. All other expenses related to the overhead rate go in the numerator. Therefore, there are many different interpretations of what is overhead and what is direct labor.

An early attempt at clarification defined direct labor as "that which changed the form or shape of the product." The definition had in it an important implication, namely that work done in converting material to some higher or more usable stage is the basic function of industry. Modern descriptions of our industrial process are stated in terms such as "conversion" and "value added."

However, the definition was lacking in two important aspects. One was that it excluded many operations that are actually direct labor. Examples are regularized inspection and packaging. The other was that it did not specify what was to be the measure of direct labor. Hence today, some accountants use labor dollars while others use labor hours. A further complication is that some accountants use dollars or hours accrued from *unmeasured* work, while others use similar bases resulting from *work measurement*. (The latter of course also has other uses when used with wage incentives.)

Consequently, the measures of direct labor (output) vary greatly from plant to plant. For instance, some treat material trucking and/or machine set-up as direct labor. In the same vein, it was at one time common practice for foremen to charge time to jobs going through their departments. On the other hand, some obviously direct costs like tumbling and heat-treating are deliberately put into overhead because their amounts are relatively insignificant. Some foundries charge the comparatively large direct cost of casting cleaning to overhead because they have not utilized convenient ways to charge costs to specific jobs.

In addition, there are mixed cases. Among these are *wait* and *extra work*. If separated, they may go into overhead. If buried in recorded times, piece work prices, or temporary rates, they go in direct labor. Similarly, there are mixed cases of materials. One example might be lumber. Boards used to make shipping boxes may

EXHIBIT I
DIFFERING OVERHEAD RATES FROM IDENTICAL DATA

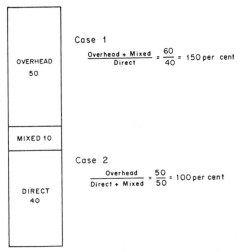

Examples of extremes in resulting overhead rates depending upon how certain expenses are classified.

be charged as direct material whereas other boards used to repair the roof are classified as indirect material and go into overhead. To summarize the effect of differing decisions about what is direct, Exhibit I shows an in-between section labelled *mixed*. Case 1 indicates an overhead percentage of 150 if all of the mixed is charged to overhead. Case 2 results in 100 percent when all mixed is classified as direct.

In Exhibit, I, the divisor is some amount representing volume for the period used in calculating the overhead rate. For this purpose, some firms use the actual volume of the recent past. This is a carryover of the practice of computing actual or job costs. The method is convenient because, presumably, actual expenses correspond with actual volume.

But volume varies from year to year. Important causes are economic weather, competitive forces, and customer response. Changes in volume cause newly determined overhead rates to vary from those previously established. Consequently, newly computed costs appear different from those formerly used for comparisons with prices and for calculating profit or loss on sales.

EXHIBIT II
TOTAL OVERHEAD
COST-VOLUME RELATIONSHIPS

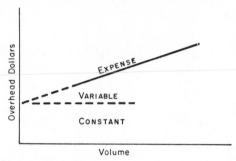

Most overhead expenses are semi-variable in that they
contain constant amounts of cost.

The reason why changes in volume affect overhead rates is that
most overhead costs are semi-variable. Exhibit II shows a typical
overhead expense. It consists of a constant plus a variable. The
same is true of total overhead, so that Exhibit II may be looked
upon as representing total overhead. Thus, there is a major total
overhead expense in a company that is fairly constant regardless
of volume. This is the cost of the nucleus of the organization of a

EXHIBIT III
PER-UNIT OVERHEAD
COST-VOLUME RELATIONSHIPS

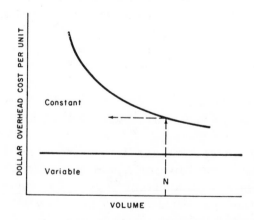

Overhead rates contain prorations of constant costs. That
is one reason why actual costs change with volume.

going concern. It includes expenses, such as depreciation, taxes, and insurance, commonly called *fixed*. The major portion, however, is made up of salaries and related costs. Because volume is divided into overhead to compute overhead rate, the amount taken as volume determines the proportion of constant cost to be assigned by the overhead rate. This is shown by Exhibit III, where the rate of constant cost is a reciprocal curve $(1/x)$. To get around such variations, some accountants elect to use calculated actual rates as standards. Other choose a standard base for volume, as 80% of capacity. A better approach is to stop the changing cost in Exhibit III by establishing a normal or standard volume, and corresponding expenses. This method is suggested by point N and usually is adopted for the purpose of computing standard costs. (See Chapter 6, STANDARD COSTING.)

It follows that variations in volume cause changes in costs and profits due simply to bookkeeping under this method, which is known as *absorption costing*. Variations in performance and in control also affect the results.

ACCOUNTING MODIFICATIONS

To separate the effects of bookkeeping from those of performance, accountants have devised several modifications. The simplest is that of adopting accounting periods of uniform length. A second way is similar in that it assigns the constant cost in relation to the proportion that one period's sales is of total anticipated annual sales. A third method is to show separately a variance due to volume.

Another relatively recent approach is variable costing (sometimes called direct costing). It begins with a separation of *direct costs* from *period costs*. In principle, direct costs are material, labor, and those portions of overhead costs that vary with production. *Period costs* are those just described as constant. The direct costs are deducted from sales income to reveal a *contribution to profit*. Then the period costs are subtracted to determine the net profit.

The advantages of variable costing can be combined with the necessities of absorption costing in one accounting system. The important reason for doing so is to determine the return on capital invested in the production and sale of each of a company's several products. This boils down to finding correct product costs.

EXHIBIT IV
ERRORS IN OVERHEAD ASSIGNMENT

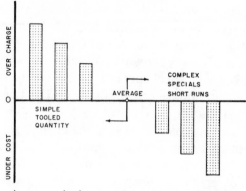

Average overhead rates tend to assign too much overhead
cost to simple products, well-tooled operations, and quantity
production and too little to complex products, special designs, and short runs. The more any of these differ from the
average product, the greater are the errors in overhead assignment.

It is in this process that there are so many variations in accounting procedures for assigning overhead costs. The reason is that a
simple average overhead rate is incorrect for non-average products.
The general types of errors are suggested by Exhibit IV. Instinctively
recognizing probable errors, some mangers have selected different
overhead rates. Often, however, such decisions are prejudiced by
desires to make costs compare more favorably with prices. (This
tendency shows through when an estimate for price quotation is
handed back with some comment like. "Sharpen your pencil.")

COST CENTERS

The usual method of breaking up an average overhead rate is to
establish departmental, cost, or burden center rates. The least
subdivision in this procedure is a machine or a workplace. In this
step, some accountants consider overhead departments as cost
centers and assign to them expenses such as heat, light, and jani-
torial. Most, however, assign overhead costs to production centers
only.

To each cost center chosen are assigned some or all of the factory expenses deemed applicable. In this sorting, some accountants separate general factory expenses from those more directly related to production. Some treat similarly any portion of a headquarters cost that is charged to a factory. Such general expenses are usually assigned to manufactured products by means of an average rate. If no such separation is made, then accountants using departmental or cost center rates charge factory expenses to those centers.

INTERRELATED FUNDAMENTALS

Underlying all of these approaches are two sets of interrelated fundamentals. These are (1) the types of costs and (2) the mechanics of overhead assignment. The types of costs are:

(a) *Cost of business done in a period of time*. This is concerned with past performance and usually is based on actual costs in that expenses such as sales and administrative, and variances from standard costs, where they exist, are written off.

(b) *Costs of existing and newly designed or proposed methods, parts, and products*. These are compiled as standard or estimated costs for predictive purposes. They are the costs managers need for comparison with current and probable prices and costs in planning the survival of the enterprise.

The mechanics of overhead assignment involve two fundamentals:

(a) *Volume used as the basis for assigning overhead costs*.

(b) *Factors chosen for making the cost assignments*.

Volume is disregarded, in effect, when a Profit & Loss statement is compiled for the recent past performance. But it has a very important bearing upon the calculation of overhead rates as portrayed in Exhibit III. Whether the volume used is the total output of a plant or a cost center, there may be errors in the resulting overhead rate because a total is used. In most companies, a total is a sum of parts that are not homogeneous. For example, sales dollars are mixtures of differing material contents, purchased or fabricated, as well as profit margins. Labor dollars are mixtures of unlike wage rates and productivities. Labor hours are mixtures of productivities and, often, times that are not direct labor, such as waiting and extra work mentioned earlier.

Further distortions in all such measures are caused by continuing changes in products, designs, methods and equipment. Such improvements, particularly those brought about by cost reduction efforts and work measurement installations, tend to reduce the volume of direct labor while increasing the related overhead expenses. All of these variations make the parts of a common denominator less alike. The basic premise of the common denominator is to obtain the equivalent of good salable pieces because the purpose is to get overhead cost per piece.

The second method may compound the mixtures just described to the extent that volumes are used to assign overhead expense to products directly, or indirectly through cost centers. Examples are prorations made on the basis of labor dollars or hours.

PRORATION

To reduce both types of errors, a different approach should be used. It recognizes that many overhead expenses are related more to the several products themselves than to any type of cost center. This is about what Peter Drucker means when he writes, "The only realistic costing of a given product is one which assumes that costs other than raw material are total costs for a period of time divided by the number of items, without regard for the volume of each item."

Therefore, generally, for complete realism, overhead costs should not be prorated on the assumption that each unit of volume is the same. Instead, each expense should be analyzed to determine its causes and their degrees. Each expense is then assigned to products according to the amounts used. For many expenses, this is done from counts or time records. As an example, the relatively large engineering costs of diversified products may be assigned to them by means of factors determined from engineering cost records. The effort is made to find a realistic way to assign each overhead expense to individual products as contrasted with using some single factor chosen as a compromise.

Thus expenses are assigned without regard to volume. This is important for two reasons. The first is that many overhead costs are like setups on production machines. They are relatively constant for a given type of sales or production order irrespective of quantity. For instance, it costs about the same to type an invoice for $35 as for $350.

Secondly, the total expense thus assigned to a product group can then be divided by the latter's own measure of volume. The conversion cost or overhead rate thus obtained would be correct for costing that product even if its measure of volume were inflated. In a simple example, suppose there are two products, A and B. Product A is made in large quantities, and its operations are on incentive. Product B is made in small lots, and, as is often the case, it is made on daywork. The productivity of Product A operations is double that of Product B operations. It takes 20 mins. to make one of A, and 40 mins. to make one item B. To keep out other variables, assume that the true overhead of either item is $1.00 each. With these figures, it is possible to build up the volume and overhead an accountant would have to start with. These are shown in the table given as Exhibit V. Common procedure is to divide the $450 total overhead by the 10,000 mins. total volume and get $.045 overhead cost per min. Overhead cost per piece is computed by multiplying $.045 by labor times as follows:

Product A: 20 mins. X $.045 = $.90 overhead assigned
Product B: 40 mins. X $.045 = $1.80 overhead assigned

If, instead, the overhead assigned to each product is divided by its measure of volume, the rate for Product A is $.050 per minute and for Product B $.025. When these product overhead rates are multiplied by their corresponding times, overhead costs are correctly assigned:

Product A: 20 mins. X $.050 = $1.00 overhead assigned
Product B: 40 mins. X $.025 = $1.00 overhead assigned

The first set of overhead assignments reflects the error of using averages. Each error causes another. The overhead not assigned to one product is applied to another as illustrated by Exhibit IV. The second set of costs shows that when overhead expenses are assigned by analysis and then are divided by volumes that are more homogeneous, the resulting costs are more correct.

It should be evident from the foregoing that there are no accurate costs. All of the various approaches are but different ways to re-

EXHIBIT V

Prod.	Quantity	Correct Over- head	Mins. Each	Volume Mins.	Overhead Cost/Min.
A	400	$400	20	8,000	$.050
B	50	50	40	2,000	.025
		$450		10,000	$.045 Av.

duce the errors in overhead assignment. All but the final method have parts of the same three errors in common. One is the use of mixed units of volume added together as though they were all alike. The second is the assignment of overhead expenses in combinations to products or cost centers. The worst cases occur when combinations are total factory overhead or total sales and administrative. The third is the proration of overhead expense. Proration presupposes the value of each unit of measure to be the same. This method disregards both the existence of constant expenses earlier described as setups, and the different degrees of overhead cost that unlike products require.

Errors in overhead costing can be reduced by doing more assigning and less prorating. This approach is applicable to either absorption or direct costing. Regardless of costing plan, it is important to show the correct relation between the price of a product and its cost to make, sell, deliver, and service. Two reasons are vital. One is that the market price level of the product will tend to be set largely by the lowest cost arrived at by the different systems of overhead.

The other is that the trend in industry is toward raising both constant and variable overhead costs by substituting better methods and equipment for some parts of direct labor. The extreme example is the completely automated plant where *everybody* is overhead. Each step taken in this direction can exaggerate errors made in overhead assignment unless more detailed analyses are used to replace simple prorations.

9

Depreciation

Depreciation concepts in business take cognizance of the fact that plants, machinery, equipment, and all types of physical assets lose value with the passage of time. There has always been a wide divergence of opinion on the subject of how rapidly equipment should be depreciated from its original installed cost to its final salvage value at the time it is to be replaced as worn out or obsoleted. Final decisions are made by experienced engineers, financial executives, and tax experts who are familiar with the particulars of the equipment and its uses.

ENGINEERING CONCEPTS

The investment in any project is determined on the basis of the amount needed for new plant and equipment, plus the cost of installing new machinery, making suitable allowances for the cost of existing machinery obsoleted by the new, as well as presently available equipment which can be transferred to the new project. Capital reserves and other temporary provisions necessary during the construction of the project should be included.

However, the decision cannot be made without careful consideration of the continuing costs of the venture. These are computed on the basis of three items: (1) interest on the money used to finance the project; (2) depreciation, the cost of equipment wearing out and becoming obsolete; and (3) expenses, including labor costs, maintenance, power, supplies, insurance, direct overhead, taxes, engineering and administrative overhead, and others.

These three items are calculated for a period of time, usually many years ahead. The resulting annual cost will be proportionally lower if depreciation is spread over a greater number of years.

The engineer's basic objective is to design and install machinery that will deliver the goods day after day, year in and year out, under severe use and abuse. His method of handling depreciation reflects this approach. If his equipment can deliver over a long life, he can claim a smaller annual cost, hence a more profitable operation.

In certain industries, there are serious dangers of forced obsolescence due to changes in types of products produced, or new methods of production, causing even unworn equipment to be abandoned to salvage. But although it is possible for the life of machinery suddenly to be cut short by forced obsolescence, it is also probable that many machines will be used long after they have depreciated completely on the accountants' books either in their original application and location or after they have been sold, salvaged, rebuilt and reinstalled. Somewhere between the extremes of forced obsolescence and extended lives of old equipment under restricted ratings is the *true life*, and this is allocated by management decision, varying with the business cycle and the type of business.

Engineers commonly use *Sinking Fund* depreciation, *Straight Line* depreciation, *Fixed Percentage* depreciation, *Machine Hours* (which would be the total running time measured by an odometer fixed to the equipment), and *Rate per Unit Output*, which is used for tools, dies, and certain manufacturing machinery which can produce only a definite number of parts before it must be replaced. (Formulas are discussed below.) Sometimes an annual rate is set up, a constant amount per year which covers the cost of depreciation and maintenance, so that as more maintenance is performed, less depreciation is taken.

When the usage of equipment will vary from year to year, depreciation may be taken in proportion to use. This permits a business to estimate its total income from a particular piece of equipment or income-producing item such as motion picture film, and take depreciation each year in proportion to income produced.

ACCOUNTING CONCEPTS

Accountants and financial experts take a point of view that is sometimes directly opposite to that of the engineers, and recommend that physical assets be written off (depreciated) as rapidly as possible. More or less depreciation can be charged "on the books" without affecting the usefulness of the plant or equipment. Thus it is possible to have the "expense" without any outlay of funds to meet the expense because the depreciating items have been paid for in past years, and additional funds are provided for the enterprise. Funds provided by depreciation charges can be invested in inventory, accounts receivable, or whatever other investments seem to encourage the greatest return on investment until again needed for replacement of equipment or other purposes.

Depreciation of physical assets is considered an expense of running the business and is therefore deducted before taxes. Since a corporation pays 20% on the first $25,000 of earnings in a year, 22% on the next $25,000, and 48% on the balance, and thus approximately 48% for large corporations in the United States (fiscal 1977), a tax deduction produces almost the same increase in income remaining after taxes as a corresponding increase in income before taxes.

Some accountants would say that no expense, depreciation or other, can lead to increase in income after taxes. For example, consider Exhibit I. Company A, which claims depreciation, has reduced net profits. On the other hand, many accountants point out that depreciation, which is lawfully claimed as tax deduction, might be higher "on the books" than in actual loss of performance

EXHIBIT I

	Company A	Company B
Profit before depreciation	$100,000	$100,000
Depreciation	10,000	None
Other tax deductions	60,000	60,000
Taxable Income	30,000	40,000
Tax at 48%	14,400	19,200
Profit after taxes	$ 15,600	$ 20,800

EXHIBIT II

	Company A	Company B
Income	$100,000	$100,000
Expenses, less depreciation	60,000	60,000
	40,000	40,000
Taxes (compilation in Exhibit I)	14,400	19,200
Funds remaining after taxes	$ 25,600	$ 20,800

or value of the equipment. So the above example might be considered another way, as shown in Exhibit II.

In this case the depreciation is an expense but not an expense involving outlay of funds. Yet it is a tax deduction and so does increase funds remaining after taxes.

Accountants may depreciate items individually, also by groups according to lives or by classes, according to use, or according to any other composite accounts. Each has its own depreciation reserve account, which is based upon the total amount invested in the group, in many cases including fully depreciated items. The value of the account and the life remaining is regularly adjusted for the retirement of assets or the acquisition of new assets, and depreciation for the group is taken according to one of the methods discussed below. It is permissible to claim accelerated deduction for tax purposes, yet keep separate books for internal business use.

DEPRECIATION FORMULAS

In the depreciation formulas here discussed, the following symbols are used:

ΔD Depreciation per year
D_x Depreciation after x years
ΔD_x Depreciation during xth year
D Total depreciation after n years
n Life of asset or group of assets, years
P Original price, total amount invested

L Lesser value, value less cost of disposing of asset after n years

B_x Book value at year x where $B_x = P - D_x$

$B_{(x-1)}$ Book value at beginning of year x

f Depreciation factor or rate

R Future replacement value

Straight Line Depreciation assumes uniform yearly depreciation from original investment, first deducting the salvage value. The formula is:

$$\Delta D = (P - L)/n$$

For example, \$15,000 invested in equipment will depreciate to \$5,000 salvage value in ten years.

$$\Delta D = (15,000 - 5,000)/10$$

$$\Delta D = \$1,000 \text{ per year}$$

$$D = \$10,000$$

Fixed Percentage Depreciation uses a depreciation percent or factor. When the difference between 100% and the factor is multiplied by itself n times (i.e., raised to the nth power), the original investment is converted to salvage value.

$$P(1.00 - f)^n = L$$

To determine the rate or factor f, the equation can be rewritten as:

$$f = 1 - (L/P)^{1/n}$$

where

$$\Delta D_1 = f \cdot P$$

and

$$\Delta D_x = f \cdot (B_{x-1})$$

Exhibit III shows the use of these formulas in an example where $P = \$16,000$, $L = \$4,000$ and n is 5 years.

Needless to say, when determining f, small salvage value must be handled with care since as L approaches zero, L/P ratio becomes

EXHIBIT III

Year	B_{x-1}	f	D	B_x
1	$16,000	.2421	3,874	$12,126
2	12,126	.2421	2,936	9,190
3	9,190	.2421	2,225	6,965
4	6,969	.2421	1,687	5,278
5	5,278	.2421	1,278	4,000

indeterminate. Notice, salvage value is not deducted before depreciation is taken.

Accountants prefer to call the fixed percentage method the *Declining Balance*, since the rate is applied to the remaining balance each year. Internal Revenue Service limits this method to twice the Straight Line Depreciation rate, which becomes a special case called *Double Declining Balance*. In a previous example we depreciated from original investment of $15,000 to $5,000 in ten years. The rate of depreciation was therefore $1,000 per year ÷ $10,000 total amount, or 10%—and so the double rate is 20%.

Double Declining Balance takes double straight line rate and applies this to each year's balance as shown in Exhibit IV.

Since it is not permissible to depreciate below the salvage value, the amounts in parentheses, theoretically correct, are not allowed. The fifth year depreciation is therefore limited to $1,144. Notice that the double rate is applied directly to original cost, and this rapid depreciation as shown above is permitted by IRS under specified conditions.

Sum of the Years (*Digits, Integers*) *Method* numbers each year, lists the numbers in inverse order, and determines the depreciation for a particular year by dividing that year's number by the sum of the digits. Exhibit V illustrates the computation. There, $14,000

EXHIBIT IV

Year	B_{x-1}	f	D	B_x
1	$15,000	.20	$3,000	$12,000
2	12,000	.20	2,400	9,600
3	9,600	.20	1,920	7,680
4	7,680	.20	1,536	6,144
5	6,144	.20	(1,229)	(4,915)
6	None permitted			

EXHIBIT V

Year	Digit	Sum of Digit Ratio	$P - L$	D	B_x
1	7	7/28	$12,000	$3,000	$9,000
2	6	6/28	12,000	2,573	6,427
3	5	5/28	12,000	2,143	4,284
4	4	4/28	12,000	1,714	2,570
5	3	3/28	12,000	1,285	1,285
6	2	2/28	12,000	857	428
7	1	1/28	12,000	428	0000
Total	28			12,000	

is depreciated over seven years with a salvage value of $2,000. Salvage is deducted first. The sum of the digits is 28, with the digits listed in inverse order. Thus, for the first year, the depreciation is $\frac{7}{28}$ of $12,000, or $3,000—and similarly for the other years.

Years of Life Remaining is an alternate method which takes the sum of the digits for any remaining years, on the balance remaining. Exhibit VI illustrates the computation, for a $15,000 investment depreciated over five years, with a salvage value of $5,000. Here, for example, the depreciation for the second year is determined by applying the sum of digits to the four years remaining, against the balance of $6,667 remaining after the depreciation for the first year has been deducted. As before, the salvage value is deducted first.

Sinking Fund Depreciation is used by engineers when it is not desirable to depreciate rapidly. It reflects the condition of a firm which is retiring indebtedness and therefore, by paying off part of the principal today, achieves the same effect as with a larger future payment. In another way we must say it anticipates that each

EXHIBIT VI

Year	Digit				f	Unre-covered $P - L$	D	B_x
1	5				5/15	10,000	3,333	11,667
2	4	4			4/10	6,667	2,688	9,000
3	3	3	3		3/6	4,000	2,000	7,000
4	2	2	2	2	2/3	2,000	1,333	5,667
5	1	1	1	1	1/1	667	667	5,000
Total	15	10	6	3				

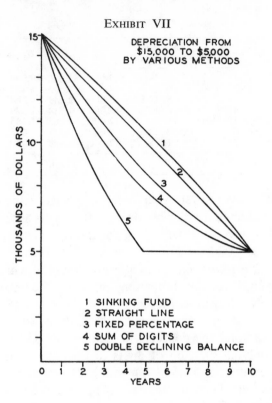

Exhibit VII

DEPRECIATION FROM
$15,000 TO $5,000
BY VARIOUS METHODS

1 SINKING FUND
2 STRAIGHT LINE
3 FIXED PERCENTAGE
4 SUM OF DIGITS
5 DOUBLE DECLINING BALANCE

credit to depreciation reserve will accumulate at compound interest to a larger future value.

Since business firms do make every effort to keep such funds working in the business to make a return, one might expect to find this method commonly used. However, business is ever changing, forced obsolescence is usually a danger, and tax considerations influence the thinking of businessmen, and so sinking fund depreciation is rarely used, and might apply more appropriately to public works and tax free institutions. In addition, most types of equipment tend to depreciate rapidly in early years and less as time goes by.

The formula is a variation of the compound interest formula:

$$D = \Delta D \left[\frac{(1 + i)^n - 1}{i} \right]$$

Values for the expression in brackets are normally listed in engineering handbooks and greatly simplify the calculation.

For example, ΔD of \$1,000 which resulted from a \$15,000 investment and \$5,000 salvage under straight line now becomes:

$$15,000 - 5,000 = \Delta D \left[\frac{(1.06)^{10} - 1}{.06} \right]$$

$$10,000 = \Delta D \times (.7908/.06)$$

$$\Delta D = \$759.00$$

This clearly shows how smaller credits to depreciation reserve under assumed conditions of 6%, compounded annually over 10 years, produce the same effect as \$1,000.00 credits and no interest assumed. Exhibit VII compares methods of depreciation graphically.

DEPRECIATION AS A TAX DEDUCTION

Since most investments are made by tax-paying firms, the consideration of depreciation usually involves its value as a tax deduction. However, this should not completely eclipse its value to engineers as an estimate of the future life of engineering projects.

Early in World War II, the U.S. Treasury Department published a schedule of acceptable useful lives, *Bulletin F*, which remained the acceptable depreciation guide for twenty years. During the tenure of this Bulletin practically every concern involved in manufacturing or similar activity using substantial capital equipment reached an agreement with IRS on special depreciation considerations, including forced obsolescence, sudden loss, abnormal retirements, and factors peculiar to the industry.

In July, 1962, recognizing that useful life varies considerably with the type of usage, and also to encourage the sale of capital equipment as a stimulus to the economy, the Treasury Department published "Depreciation Guidelines and Rules" *Publication No. 456*, also called Revenue Procedure 62-21, which grouped properties and equipment into types of business. This shortened depreciable life from an average of nineteen years under the old *Bulletin F* to thirteen years for all manufacturing industry. It was still optional for a taxpayer to group his assets into the guideline classes. The guidelines contained a reserve ratio test to permit depreciation allowances to exceed the newly published rules. The ratio was the depreciation reserve times 100, divided by the cost of all assets, then multiplied by a rate of growth calculated as present assets divided by their value in the original or base year.

In 1968 the Federal Government conducted a computer simulation which attempted to determine if the reserve ratio test was indeed an accurate check showing that the depreciation tax deductions taken by the taxpayers were accurately reflecting their actual investments in new equipment, and were serving the intended purpose of stimulating economic growth in this country.

In general, the taxpayers tended to claim depreciation tax deductions without corresponding investment. Also, a problem developed when the new guidelines were used together with certain methods of depreciation (sum of digits), giving some taxpayers unjustified benefits. Because of this, Revenue Procedure 65-13 extended the moratorium on the reserve ratio test, and Revenue Procedure 72-10 in 1971 permitted the new ADR system, described below, with no reserve ratio test at all.

Because of the faster rates negotiated individually by businessmen under the old rules, these rates were greeted with some degree of skepticism, but the Treasury Department estimated that it would lose $1\frac{1}{2}$ billion in tax revenue during the first full year of operation under these rules. In subsequent years the stimulation of tax relief could result in greater prosperity and subsequently greater tax revenues. Each purchase of capital goods contains a multiplier effect. As business picks up for the seller of capital goods, he in turn purchases more resources, and a chain reaction, the "multiplier effect," sets in, subject to taxes at every step. Theoretically the multiplier is small but the psychological implications are great.

Interest on indebtedness is also a tax deduction, and it might appear that it would be equally advantageous to operate under increased debt, but unlike depreciation, interest payments must be met. It is possible for depreciation to take place on the books, often an accelerated depreciation taken for tax purposes only, while the true decline in value of the machinery or equipment may require no payments whatsoever, or deferred payments. Sudden losses and rapid retirements are handled by additional deductions if the situation so permits.

Depreciation allowances and allowances for interest paid on indebtedness may take place at the same time for the same taxpayer, resulting in a greater combined tax saving.

Many items lose value rapidly in the first year simply because they enter the "used" category. IRS permits an extra 20% depreciation allowance up to $2,000 maximum deduction ($10,000 maximum expenditure) during the first year, in addition to the normally calculated depreciation.

The entire 20% allowance may be taken in the first year regardless of salvage, providing the item was tangible property having a useful life of at least six years and in use for part of the year. The usual depreciation methods, including the rapid double declining balance, can be used at the same time but only for the fractional part of the year that the item or group of items was in use.

The fast double declining balance method is limited to new equipment purchased after 1953, whereas 150% (wherein f equals $1\frac{1}{2}$ times straight line percentage) is the limit for used assets or assets purchased in 1953 or earlier. In the case of real estate other than low-income housing, the date is July 26, 1969 rather than 1953.

How is it an advantage for a business to claim tax savings from depreciation in present years rather than in the future? Highly competitive businessmen, concerned about the ever present dangers of obsolescence and the uncertainty of future business, consider today's income vital. Any savings made today results in funds that can be reinvested at compound interest, and in many concerns the best reinvestment is to carry additional assets in inventory, accounts receivable, property and equipment, or whatever makes the operation more efficient.

Consider the savings of $100,000 depreciation in chemical equipment. Under *Bulletin F* the life was fifteen to twenty-two years. Under *Guideline* classes, the life became eleven years. Using straight line depreciation the amounts are $(100,000/15) = $6,660$ per year, and $(100,000/11) = $9,090$ per year. The difference, $2,430, is additional tax deduction, and at a 48% tax rate, the saving is $1,166 per year. If the project were simply operated to the end of its useful life and abandoned, the total depreciation would seem to be the same in either case. However, consider the time value of money:

The formula to compare present values of yearly investments is:

$$P = R \left[\frac{1 - (1 + i)^n}{i} \right]$$

where i = interest or rate of return, the R rent or yearly amount. The present value of $6,660 per year for fifteen years at 10% (after taxes) is $50,000, while for $9,090 per year for eleven years it is $59,000; and 48% of the difference is $4,320, today's value of the accumulated savings. Of course, if future values are used, the amount is correspondingly greater, as a result of the compound interest effect. In the above case, the amounts after fifteen years compounded at 10% would be $210,500 and $245,800; and 48% of the difference would be $16,944.

In the same way, the advantage of accelerated depreciation over slower methods could be demonstrated to produce a saving, both in the long run and in the short run.

Exceptions are rare, but occasionally a firm may expect greater future earnings, and in such case it would be an advantage to take less depreciation at present so as to save tax deductions for future periods when income is higher. IRS permits users of declining balance depreciation to switch over to the slower straight line method on the remaining balance whenever they so elect, without permission.

The advantage of rapid depreciation almost seems to be lost when assets are grouped, since the older items in the group depress the group average. Nevertheless, the amount to be gained in the early life of the asset should, by virtue of compound interest, have a greater long-run effect.

When items are grouped into an average life class, the taxpayer may lose the advantage of a fast write-off on some items in the group. For example, consider one group of four machines. These depreciate $2,500 each per year on a straight-line basis. The group life is four years. On a straight-line basis, the first year's depreciation would be $10,000. Now, what happens when we do not group these items? Let us assume the actual lives of these four items are three, four, four, and five years. The respective depreciation amounts would be $3,333, $2,500, $2,500, and $2,000. In the latter case the depreciation is a total of $10,333 per year for the first three years, whereas it was only $10,000 per year for the same items when they were grouped.

For all of the methods of depreciation described here (excepting the sinking fund), the principle holds true, all else being equal, that grouping the items results in less depreciation in the early years.

ASSET DEPRECIATION RANGE (ADR)

This is a system adopted in 1971 by the Internal Revenue Service which allows the taxpayer to group his assets by year placed in service (vintage accounts), or to keep them in item accounts and to base his depreciation on any period of years selected by the taxpayer within a range specified for designated classes of assets. The range, approximately "guideline lives" plus and minus 20%, has been published in Revenue Procedures as contained in Section 109 of the Revenue Act of 1971, and generally liberalized over the years. Taxpayers may elect the new ADR system (which requires no reserve ratio test at all) only on assets acquired in 1971 or later. The acquisitions must be scheduled with the taxpayers' return, so that IRS can decide if they properly belong to that particular asset group. The approved group then can be depreciated according to the life range published for that particular group.

Each asset group is entitled to an allowance for repairs which is tax deductible in the same period of time, as an "expensed" item.

Salvage values are set and not adjusted unless actual practice is too far off target, i.e., more than 10% low. Salvage value is not taken into account in establishing the annual depreciation deduction for an asset or class of assets, but no assets may be depreciated below their salvage value. Grouping for depreciation is a simple, effective way of handling things, but once a grouping is established as approved by IRS, then it is "all or none." IRS will not permit exceptions, although certain real estate properties have special rules in this regard.

BONUS DEPRECIATION

This depreciation is allowed during the first year in which depreciation is claimed on any item or group of items considered "tangible personal property." The bonus allows the taxpayer an additional deduction in the amount 20% of the cost of the investment to a maximum amount of $2,000 tax deduction. Twenty per cent of the total "costs" is permitted, regardless of any expected future salvage values and regardless of the life of the items claimed (six year minimum). The remaining cost, after reduction for the bonus depreciation, may be depreciated under any of the methods acceptable to the Federal Government.

REPLACEMENT ACCOUNTING

Changes in the marketplace for assets cause historical costs to become untrue; for example, an older established industry with minimal changes over the years which is pricing its product based on historical cost data may be unknowingly liquidating its manufacturing facilities because it will not be able to replace them. In 1976, after years of rapid changes, the Securities Exchange Commission required for the first time that a corporation's annual report must reflect the replacement value of the corporation's physical assets.

While the S.E.C. asked for an evaluation of assets at current price levels, an engineer would calculate replacement value by obtaining an up-to-date price for the asset and adding current installation costs, considering possible salvage value or demolition costs as part of the installation cost. If the asset is currently useful, the years of remaining life are estimated and the total future replacement value is "brought back" to today's replacement value by the compound interest formula, $B = R/(1 + i)^{n-x}$ where $n - x$

is the years remaining. The interest rate, i, may or may not be corrected for the effects of inflation and alternate uses for funds.

In periods of high inflation it is not unusual that some assets actually appreciate in value rather than depreciate. But at the same time the attrition in normal usage of other assets, coupled with inflation of replacement prices, is causing a significant spread.

The law of supply and demand affects each particular asset's replacement value. For one example, a production machine price may increase severalfold if it was once a mass produced item but now becomes a specialty because of lack of demand. Technological innovations, as in the field of electronics and calculators, can cause prices to tumble, as when circuitry is improved and manufacturing breakthroughs develop. Competitive innovations may obsolete a manufacturing process which can only be effectively replaced by an investment much different from what historical costs might have indicated.

Considering these facts, we can conclude that a statement of replacement value is more of an art than a science and is a reflection of management's honest and considered opinion of predicted values in the field served by each corporation. The engineering estimate would be accurate only where the effects of obsolescense, supply and demand, innovations, governmental incentives, etc. are minimal, but is always a useful tool for managerial purposes.

INVESTMENT CREDIT

The Revenue Act of 1962 included a measure to stimulate the economy by tax relief on capital equipment, not including property and buildings. A businessman would calculate his income tax by the usual method, and then deduct from his tax an amount equal to 7% of his current investment.

Investment credit at the present time is 10% for items with ten years of life, two thirds of that for items with five to seven years, and one third for items with three to five years. This amount is a permissible deduction from income tax due, instead of being deducted before taxes are calculated, but may be taken only once for each investment.

Tax considerations are an important reason why depreciation is usually treated from an accounting standpoint in business literature. However, it should not be neglected as an engineering tool to help understand the effect of equipment life upon the annual cost or capitalization required of engineering projects such as public works which may be exempt from tax considerations.

10
Budgeting

Budgeting is an important—and, in any operation of significant size and complexity, an indispensable—part of management planning and control. Its objectives are three-fold: (1) to determine the input of planning, in terms of the costs of agreed upon activities and expectable levels of those activities, as well as expected revenues, if any, resulting from those activities; (2) to warn decision-makers and responsible managers when significant departures from planned cost inputs and revenues occur; and (3) to develop a responsive, cooperative workforce in the matter of fiscal control.

A comprehensive budget may be defined as a forecast of all of the transactions of an organization for a stipulated period, organized in such a way as to bring to the attention of specific managers the financial results of those activities over which they have control, and to enable the preparation of financial statements such as the budgeted income statement, balance sheet, and cash flow statement.

The budgeting process itself is an extensive one, and consists of the preparation of individual budgets by those departments (or persons) best in a position to do so—for example, the sales budget by the sales department, the production budget by the production department, the purchases budget by the purchasing agent, and so on. The preparation of some of these budgets, for example, the manufacturing overhead and selling expense budgets, is expedited by a well developed system of flexible budgets. Standard cost data are also of help in providing information as to hours or quantities needed for manufacture at any given level of activity. In turn, the budgeting process itself may lead to the revision of flexible budgets and the updating of standard costs.

The timing and detailed preparation of each of the various budgets which in total form the master budget are usually the responsibility of a budget director, who in turn may have the help and authoritative back-up of a budget committee. The budget committee may be composed of the top executives of the firm, including the president, controller, and budget director.

I—FLEXIBLE BUDGETING

Flexible Budgeting is a major technique of cost control which may be employed whether or not a formal system of standard costs is in use, but is commonly closely integrated with the operation of a company's standard cost system. The flexible budget sets expense allowances for stated levels of output. These serve as a guide as to what costs *should be* at an *achieved* level of output, and how costs should change when output diminishes or increases.

Flexible budgets may be established for any component of expense—manufacturing, selling, administrative—and for any level of supervision. An example of a flexible budget which indicates costs by activity levels is shown in Exhibit I.

Another method of flexible budget presentation stemming out of either scatter diagram or least squares analysis, and stressing a careful separation of fixed and variable costs, is shown in Exhibit II. (The same data employed in Exhibit I are used in this illustration.)

FIXED AND VARIABLE EXPENSE ANALYSIS

Flexible budgets involve the division of expense items into variable, fixed, and "mixed," and a subsequent analysis of the "mixed" expenses into their fixed and variable elements by a study of their reaction to changes in operational activity.

Mixed expenses may be related to changing levels of output simply through the use of experienced but subjective judgment. On the other hand, a study may be made of these expenses by means of scatter diagram or least squares analysis. In either of the latter cases, past experience in terms of dollars spent at actual levels of output achieved is arrayed and studied, non-random variations are

EXHIBIT I

FLEXIBLE BUDGET SHOWING COSTS BY LEVELS OF OUTPUT
Department No. 16

Expense	Direct Labor Hours					
	40,000	50,000	60,000	70,000	80,000	90,000
Indirect Materials	$1,000	$1,250	$1,500	$ 1,750	$ 2,000	$ 2,250
Power	400	500	600	700	800	900
Indirect Labor	1,800	2,200	2,600	3,000	3,400	3,800
Maintenance	300	350	400	450	500	550
Supplies	550	650	750	850	950	1,050
Miscellaneous	950	1,100	1,250	1,400	1,550	1,700
Depreciation	500	500	500	500	500	500
Space Occupancy	400	400	400	400	400	400
Supervision	1,000	1,000	1,000	1,000	1,000	1,000
Totals	$6,900	$7,950	$9,000	$10,050	$11,100	$12,150

EXHIBIT II

FLEXIBLE BUDGET SHOWING COSTS BY
FIXED AND VARIABLE ELEMENTS
Department No. 16

	Fixed Amount (if any)	Variable Rate
Indirect Materials		$0.025
Power		.010
Indirect Labor	$ 200	.040
Maintenance	100	.005
Supplies	150	.010
Miscellaneous	350	.015
Depreciation	500	
Space Occupancy	400	
Supervision	1,000	
Totals	$2,700	$0.105

eliminated, and the behavior of the remaining items are generalized on a straight-line basis.

Scatter Diagram Analysis of a Mixed Expense.   The data in Exhibit III represent a company's historical experience with indirect labor cost. These figures are plotted graphically in Exhibit IV to illustrate the use of scatter diagram analysis to effect the separation of a mixed expense into its fixed and variable elements.

Note that the cost curve intersects the vertical axis at about $51,000, indicating the fixed element of indirect labor cost. Once this amount is known, total indirect labor cost for some one

EXHIBIT III

HISTORICAL DATA FOR MIXED EXPENSE ANALYSIS

Month	Direct Labor Hours	Indirect Labor Cost
January	65,000	$70,000
February	70,000	68,000
March	40,000	62,000
April	40,000	63,000
May	50,000	67,000
June	75,000	75,000
July	66,000	65,000
August	65,600	69,300
September	70,000	74,000
October	90,000	78,000
November	82,000	74,000
December	75,000	70,000

EXHIBIT IV

SCATTER DIAGRAM ANALYSIS OF INDIRECT LABOR COST

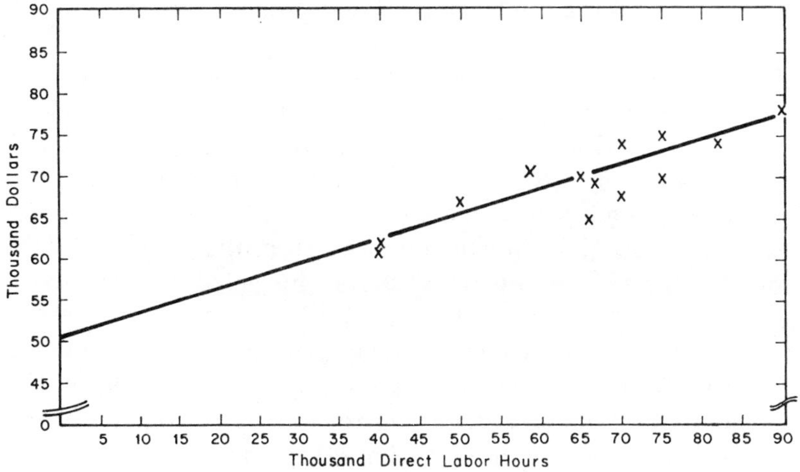

particular level of output is estimated from the cost curve, for example, indirect labor cost at 10,000 direct labor hours totals $54,000. To obtain the variable rate per direct labor hour, fixed indirect labor cost of $51,000 just noted is subtracted from the $54,000 total indirect labor cost, and divided by 10,000 direct labor hours. The variable rate for indirect labor cost is therefore $0.30 per direct labor hour. These data may be summarized and generalized into a formula for indirect labor cost, where Y represents indirect labor cost, a, the fixed element in indirect labor cost, b, the rate in dollars and cents at which indirect labor cost varies with changes in activity, and x the measurement of activity:

$$Y = a + bx$$

Indirect labor cost data as analyzed in the foregoing example may be shown therefore as:

Indirect labor cost = $51,000 + $0.30x

Horngren, in "Cost Accounting," Chapter 25, presents a comprehensive discussion of the application of least squares analysis, a mathematical and statistical approach to the separation of mixed expenses into their fixed and variable elements[1]. A sophisticated discussion concerning a wide variety of cost behaviors expressible in cost equations is given by Dopuch and Birnberg, "Cost Accounting."[2]

Flexible budgeting may be used as a basis for performance control over any specified area of business operations. For example, if Department No. 16 referred to in Exhibits I and II incurred $10,600 expenses when operating at 60,000 direct labor hours (DLH), the flexible budget given in either Exhibit I or II is used as a basis for determining variations in expense items from that allowed by the budget. Exhibit V presents the actual and budgeted costs of Department No 16 for the month of November.

Control procedures would call for an explanation of the variance of $1,600. Such an explanation is facilitated when (1) the budget is separated into expense items controllable by the supervisor and those which are not, with correction efforts directed toward controllable items, or (2) flexible budgeting for overhead costs is integrated into either overhead accounting or standard costing, and the overhead variance is analyzed into controllable and non-controllable variances.

FLEXIBLE BUDGETING AND OVERHEAD ACCOUNTING

When a flexible budget is employed in conjunction with overhead accounting, the budget is used to construct overhead rates which are in turn used to apply overhead costs to production. Differences between actual and applied overhead may in such instance be analyzed into (1) a variance deemed *controllable by the supervisor*, called a budget, performance, or expense variance, and (2) a variance denoting the *inability of top management to provide work*, called a capacity, volume, or activity variance.

To illustrate the computation and use of these variances, assume that the fixed overhead rate is based on an average monthly output of 60,000 DLH. Dividing the $2,700 fixed overhead cost obtained

---

[1]Horngren, Charles T., "Cost Accounting," Englewood Cliffs, N.J., Prentice-Hall, 4th ed., 1977.

[2]Dopuch, Nicholas, and Birnberg, Jacob G., "Cost Accounting: Accounting Data for Management Decisions," New York, Harcourt, Brace & Jovanovitch, 1969.

from Exhibit II by 60,000, the fixed cost rate per DLH become $0.045. The variable overhead rate obtainable from the same Exhibit II is $0.105 per DLH. During November, when Department No. 16 works 50,000 DLH, manufacturing overhead incurred and overhead costs applied to production are pictured in the "T" accounts given in Exhibit VI.

In the 2-variance method of analysis (in a non-standard cost system), the analyst would separate the difference between the $8,200 spent and the $7,500 taken to inventories into two variances. He would first turn to the budget of overhead cost allowed for 50,000 DLH, $7,950 (see Exhibit I), and subtract it from the actual manufacturing overhead costs of $8,200. The resulting variance of $250 would ordinarily be typed as a *controllable* budget variance and, if considered significant, would require explanation ·from the supervisor and subsequent efforts at correction.

In turn, the analyst would compare the $7,950 allowed overhead cost with the $7,500 applied to output (see "T" accounts, Exhibit VI), and compute a capacity variance of $450. (To check: multiply 10,000 DLH worked below average capacity times the fixed cost rate of $0.045.) This variance is ordinarily interpreted as resulting from management's inability to obtain sufficient orders to keep the department busy, and, if so, it would be charged as a cost of

EXHIBIT V

ACTUAL AND BUDGETED COSTS OF
DEPARTMENT NO. 16
November, 19—

	Budget for 60,000 DLH	Actual Costs	Variance
Indirect Materials	$1,500	$ 2,000	$ 500
Power	600	550	(50)
Indirect Labor	2,600	3,000	400
Maintenance	400	700	300
Supplies	750	950	200
Miscellaneous	1,250	1,500	250
Depreciation	500	500	
Space Occupancy	400	400	
Supervision	1,000	1,000	
Totals	$9,000	$10,600	$1,600

general administration rather than a variance controllable by the supervisor of Department No 16. However, alternatively, failure to utilize facilities at normal in Department No. 16 may have been due to inefficiency and work stoppages in previous departments, requiring lay-offs in Department No. 16. In this latter instance, therefore, the variance becomes the responsibility of supervision taking place prior to Department No. 16.

FLEXIBLE BUDGETING AND STANDARD COSTING

If carefully developed, the flexible budgets described in Exhibits I and II could also be used in standard costing. In standard costing, under a 2-variance method of analysis, a subtle change would take place in the construction of the fixed overhead rate. Normal capacity would refer to good output achieved, not actual hours worked. In addition, standard overhead rates would be applied to hours *allowed* for good output achieved rather than actual hours. For example, assume that in the preceding illustration, 60,000 *actual* direct labor hours had been worked, but that only 50,000 "standard direct labor hours of output" were earned. The 25,000 units of product manufactured were allowed only 2 hours of direct labor time each at standard. Despite the fact that 60,000 DLH were worked, all figures to be shown in "T" accounts and the derivation of resulting variances would remain the same as in the foregoing illustration based upon 50,000 DLH. The budget allowance of $7,950 would be based upon 50,000 DLH earned, and the capacity variance would be computed by comparing the 50,000 DLH earned with the stated normal of 60,000 DLH.

In discussing defects in commonly used methods of overhead variance analysis when used in connection with flexible budgeting, critics have complained that so-called controllable budget variances are often caused by a variety of dissimilar events having little relationship to one another. The magnitude of the budget variance, for example, is often affected by prices paid for expense factors not always controllable by a supervisor, by inefficient use of expense items such as supplies and power, and, in standard costing, by excessive use of time calling for increased operating expenses. If the "T" account data in Exhibit VI were based on standard

EXHIBIT VI

OVERHEAD ACCOUNTS

Mfg. Oh. Dept. No. 16	Work in Process
Actual	From Mfg.
$8,200	Oh. Applied
	$7,500

Mfg. Oh. Dept. No. 16 Applied

To Work in Proc.
(50,000 × $0.15)
$7,500

costs and 60,000 DLH had been operated, one might argue that the supervisor of Department No. 16 did quite well. If the budget allowance were based upon the 60,000 actual hours worked, the supervisor would have been allowed $9,000 overhead cost (see Exhibit I), and he had only spent $8,200. Futhermore, the capacity variance of $450, often termed uncontrollable by lower level supervision, is in this instance indicative of the use of exessive time in the achievement of output.

Improvement in Variance Analysis Through Use of the 3-Variance Method. When flexible budgeting is utilized in connection with standard costing, use of a 3-variance method of analysis overcomes some of the objections noted in the use of the 2-variance method. The budget is based on actual hours worked, and the effect of the excessive use of time or saving in time on the total overhead variance is separated into a variance called an "efficiency" variance. Normal capacity continues to be based upon standard hours earned.

To illustrate, using the same data employed in the "T" accounts in Exhibit VI, actual manufacturing overhead cost for November is $8,200, and standard overhead cost applied to products is $7,500. A revised budget variance is computed on the basis of 60,000 actual direct labor hours worked ($8,200 actual overhead—$9,000 overhead allowed), and a favorable budget variance of $800 results. The efficiency variance is computed by multiplying the 10,000 extra hours taken (60,000 DLH actual—50,000 DLH allowed) by the variable overhead rate of $0.105. This would give an unfavorable efficiency variance of $1,050. In accountancy, the $1,050 unfavorable amount would be carried as a debit variance. Were less hours utilized than were allowed, the efficiency variance would denote a favorable use of time, and the variance would be shown as a credit. The capacity variance would be computed as under the 2-variance method above to be $450. In this illustration, therefore, the total variance of $700 ($8,200 actual less $7,500 standard) has analyzed into a favorable budget variance of $800, an unfavorable efficiency variance of $1,050, and an unfavorable capacity variance of $450.

It should be emphasized at this point that none of the variances calculated are self-explanatory. They require further investigation to determine their cause. As was pointed out earlier, changes in factor prices may affect the amount of the budget variance. Excessive use of time as expressed by an efficiency variance may be laid to lack control in the current department; but on the other hand, they may be indicative of defective or off-grade materials and delays due to difficulties in other departments.

II—RESPONSIBILITY REPORTING

Responsibility Reporting is a term used to describe accounting and management reporting systems that are directed toward controlling costs at basic supervisory levels. It is a primary management control tool and an essential companion to the delegation of authority by management. Formally defined, responsibility reporting involves a grouping and defining of the responsibilties within an organization structure, the determination and assignment of costs to appropriate levels and activities, and a strong emphasis on cost controllability.

APPROACHES AND TECHNIQUES

Responsibility reporting does not introduce new techniques to accounting practice. It does, however, provide a convenient means of presenting to management an important concept of accounting. Under responsibility reporting, the organization of responsibilities, the accounting for costs, and the budgetary control operations are integrated into one overall program to serve management.

Decentralization and delegation of management authority and

responsibility create the need for developing a responsibility reporting system. Decentralization also provides a real though not insurmountable obstacle to the design of the system. The problem is that true decentralization of responsibility requires parallel authority, which often extends to freedom in internal organization. Responsibility reporting seeks to establish a reporting structure directly related to the organization structure. If each level has authority to define its own internal organization, the organization structure tends to become both nonuniform and nonstatic. Under such circumstances it is not practical to attempt a standardization of the system of accounts, responsibilities for accounts, and management reports.

In many cases involving decentralized management, the only workable approach to responsibility reporting (other than a company reorganization) is to develop a system for general application by each subdivision of the organization to its own operations. *Each level of management defines and assigns responsibilities and reporting systems for the next lower level only*. The definition of content and the application of the chart of accounts, aside from determining responsibilities, can and should be standardized and controlled at the top level of management. However, such a chart of accounts should not be prepared in a way that would force a particular type of organization on each subdivision.

In some situations, a well defined and standardized organization exists at all levels of management. Here the system design can be specific. Responsibilities for accounts can be definitely assigned and standard reports can be prepared for all positions of responsibility.

In any case, whether or not the organization is standardized, certain principles of good organization must be followed. Those principles which are important to the responsibility reporting program are: (1) every necessary function is assigned to a unit of organization; (2) the assignment of responsibilities is specific and understood; (3) overlapping of responsibilities must not exist; (4) each position of an organization reports to one and only one supervisor; and (5) a supervisory position over each logical grouping (either geographic or functional) of activities at each management level must be assigned.

For economy and personality reasons, no actual organization

follows the ideal. Situations where one person occupies several different positions of responsibility are handled by separately identifying each position. It is then established that the one person has several separate and distinct official positions. For example, in one division a manager may be responsible for both sales and advertising, while in another division a separate manager may head up each of these functional areas. These positions are reported as separate responsibilities, and the flow of reports for summarization purposes follows its own separate functional responsibility channel. Thus, in the one case the manager might receive two summary reports—one for the sales area and the other for advertising. In the second case the two reports would be separately directed to the two managers. By focusing attention on functions and functional organization, flexibility of application is retained to fit actual organization and assignment of responsibilities.

RELATION TO COST ACCOUNTING

Responsibility reporting is closely associated with cost accounting. Certainly a cost accounting system which is to be used as a managing tool must first assign responsibility for expenses. This is particularly true in standard cost systems. Knowledge of variances in performance has little meaning if responsibility for these variances is not established. While it is entirely possible to establish a responsibility reporting system which is not intended to produce product costing, a good all-purpose system will incorporate the essential principles of product cost accounting.

The design of responsibility reporting systems should be guided by the same rules applied to cost accounting. Some of the more significant principles are: (1) appropriate accounts should be established so that cost items can be readily recorded in the proper account without detailed analysis, cost items can be kept intact, and each account represents a homogeneous, well defined, and readily analyzed expense grouping without reconstruction of accounts; (2) all items of expense should be recorded according to the lowest level or area of operations to which they can be directly related and assigned; (3) no items should be split to a lower classification requiring allocation or proration on any basis, however appropriate; and (4) any desired information which requires cost allocations or other arbitrary assignment of costs to lower levels of classification should be provided only by special analytical reports prepared from basic accounting records.

RELATION TO BUDGETING

Responsibility reporting is essential to the most effective use of budgetary control. A definition of responsibilities for the budget is the first step in preparing a budget. If the budget performance is to be reported and measured, the accounting system must coincide with established budgetary responsibilities. While it is possible to have responsibility reporting without a budget program, an effective budget cannot be established practically without a responsibility reporting system.

A necessary requirement of a responsibility reporting system designed to support a budget program is complete coordination of the two. Responsibility reporting system design should be guided by the following budgeting rules: (1) budget (and all types of responsibility) performance accounting and reporting should be tied directly to actual financial accounting without memo adjustments or additions; (2) budgets should be directed toward the control of expenditures at the point of disbursements approval; and (3) budgets should be simple and confined to the main purpose.

SAMPLE REPORTS

The following sample reports illustrate how some of the key features of responsibility reporting work in a typical manufacturing company. Each executive and supervisor in the company's organization has his own report, reflecting items of income and expense over which he has control.

Exhibit I shows the costs chargeable to the foreman of the Punch-Press Department for the current month and for the year to date, as well as variances above and below the foreman's budget. Associated reports for each succeeding higher level of organizational responsibility are also shown in Exhibits II, III, and IV.

The Punch-Press foreman is held fully responsible for the costs

EXHIBIT I
THE TYPICAL COMPANY
PUNCH PRESS DEPARTMENT
O. A. Belforth, Foreman   May, 1973
COST REPORT

Year to Date			Current Month	
Actual	Gain (Loss)		Actual	Gain (Loss)
$ 87,500	$ (7,000)	Direct Labor	$15,600	$(1,200)
4,000	(400)	Rework Labor	900	(150)
14,800	(2,700)	Indirect Labor	2,500	(500)
22,900	(4,050)	Overtime Premium	1,300	(100)
3,400	50	Supervision	650	—
5,100	1,100	Operating Supplies	1,000	200
7,000	500	Spoilage	1,400	100
3,500	(2,000)	Other	650	(350)
$148,200	$(14,500)	Total	$24,000	$(2,000)

given in his report, since they represent the usage of labor, materials, and supplies over which he has authority. The designations "supervision" refers to his own salary and the salaries of supervisors reporting to him.

It should be noted that both fixed and variable costs are included in this report without distinction, although controllable costs could be so shown (see Exhibit V in Section I-FLEXIBLE BUDGETING, in this chapter.) The test is whether these costs are controllable by the foreman. He has, for example, the power to decide how many people to keep on his department's payroll and how much overtime is needed to get the work done on time. Even if these decisions must be reviewed at higher levels, the basic authority and responsibility are his. (If they are not, these expenses should not be charged to his account, but to the account of the executive who actually has the decision-making power in each case.)

For consistency throughout the reporting structure, the heading "Gain (Loss)" is used instead of the more common "Over (Under) Standard" or "Increase (Decrease)." "Gain" always means a variation that is favorable to profits; "Loss" always means a variation that is unfavorable.

In Exhibit II, the totals for the Punch-Press Department—both

EXHIBIT II

THE TYPICAL COMPANY

PRODUCTION DEPARTMENT

D. F. Colhart, Superintendent   May, 1973

COST REPORT

Year to Date			Current Month	
Actual	Gain (Loss)		Actual	Gain (Loss)
$ 8,200	$ 1,300	Superintendent's Office	$ 1,500	$ 200
78,600	5,100	Shearing and Slitting	16,300	1,000
49,500	1,100	Screw Machine	9,600	200
58,000	2,100	Drill Press	11,800	400
148,200	(14,500)	Punch-Press	24,000	(2,000)
34,800	2,100	Welding	6,800	400
93,000	(2,200)	Finishing	18,000	(700)
96,500	(6,200)	Assembly	20,000	1,400
$566,800	$(11,200)	Total	$108,000	$ 900

EXHIBIT III

THE TYPICAL COMPANY

MANUFACTURING

G. N. Horner, Vice-President, Manufacturing

May, 1973

COST REPORT

Year to Date			Current Month	
Actual	Gain (Loss)		Actual	Gain (Loss)
$ 14,700	$ 700	Vice-President's Office	$ 2,650	$ 150
32,000	2,500	Plant Maintenance	6,000	450
32,000	900	Tool and Die Shop	7,200	200
10,000	(1,200)	Production Control	2,500	(200)
566,800	(11,200)	Production	108,000	900
22,500	50	Inspection and Quality Control	4,900	160
10,000	350	Purchasing	2,100	60
22,500	1,000	Receiving, Stores, and Shipping	3,800	250
$710,500	$ (6,900)	Total	$137,150	$ 1,970

EXHIBIT IV
THE TYPICAL COMPANY
INCOME AND EXPENSE STATEMENT

May, 1973

	Year to Date		Current Month	
	Actual	*Gain (Loss)*	*Actual*	*Gain (Loss)*
Net Sales	$1,610,000	$(20,000)	$340,000	$(3,000)
Cost of Sales	1,243,500	(9,000)	277,200	(6,200)
Manufacturing Cost Variances	6,900	(6,900)	(1,970)	1,970
Gross Profit	$ 359,600	$(35,900)	$ 64,770	$(7,230)
SELLING, GENERAL AND ADMINISTRATIVE				
Engineering	$ 60,100	500	$ 12,500	$ 300
Sales	190,600	(1,300)	21,050	100
Finance	43,000	900	8,300	100
Personnel	14,500	400	3,500	180
President's Office	15,500	1,100	3,600	250
Total	233,700	1,600	48,950	930
Net Profit—Before Income Taxes	$ 125,900	$(34,300)	$ 15,820	$(6,300)

actual and variance from the budget—are carried to the report for the foreman's immediate supervisor, the production superintendent. This report also shows total expenses for which each of the other foremen supervised by the superintendent is responsible. Normally, the superintendent will also receive copies of the more detailed reports given to his subordinates; he also receives a complete statement of the expenses chargeable directly to his own department (supervision, secretarial, space, etc.), broken down like those for the organizational units under him.

The Manufacturing Vice-President's Report (Exhibit III) summarizes the results reported to the Production Department and the other departments for which he is responsible, as well as the expenses of his own office that cannot be fairly assigned to any of those subordinates.

Exhibit IV, the income and expense statement, is the President's Report. It summarizes the costs incurred by the Manufacturing, Sales, Engineering, Finance, and Personnel groups, plus the president's own costs.

INSTALLATION

The design and installation of a responsibility reporting program represents a major undertaking, requiring competence in solving problems in organization, cost accounting, budgeting, and cost control. But more important than technical competence is the participation of general management. This participation must begin immediately with a clarification of the organization and assignment of responsibilities, and continue through the installation and administration of the program. In doing this, general management must be extremely careful not to assume the roles of the accountant or systems designer. Each decision must be examined in relation to good accounting practice and practical system operation. By emphasizing the part that the operating manager and the accountant play, the program makes necessary a team effort.

Financial management is ordinarily assigned the responsibility for the technical development of the system. This includes conducting detailed field surveys, designing a coding system for a chart of accounts and responsibility identification, preparing a manual of accounts, designing detailed procedures, issuing a manual of instructions, and accomplishing the installation of the system. It further includes calling to the attention of general management organizational inconsistencies that come to light during the study.

A thorough understanding of the operations as conducted in the field is essential to designing the system. This is gained from an extensive survey of all areas of operating and administrative activity. In this survey, emphasis must be placed on identifying costs, origins of costs, authority for approval of expenditures, management responsibilities for operations, and organization structures for responsibilties. This information must be sufficient to describe the organization structure as to chain of command, groupings of responsibilities and levels of management; to prepare a chart and descriptive manual of accounts; to develop management reports; and to develop necessary procedures and instructions.

APPLICABILITY OF RESPONSIBILITY REPORTING

Over the years, management's attention has been increasingly directed toward the refinement and usage of accounting and financial tools as operating tools. Organization principles, cost accounting systems, and budgetary cost controls were developed to a highly useful state. With these techniques already developed, whenever the need for accounting controls is recognized, it is now possible to integrate them into a single package under the title of responsibility reporting.

The concept of responsibility reporting is extremely important for the control of all types of organized effort. It has been applied with great success in every type of business activity. Responsibility reporting is a basic tool for effective management control in all companies.

III—ZERO-BASE BUDGETING

Zero-base budgeting became a "buzzword" in management circles ever since President Carter, upon assuming office in January of 1977, announced that he was setting the future Federal budgeting process on the concepts set forth in "Zero-Base Budgeting: A Practical Management Tool for Evaluating Expenses," by Peter A. Pyhrr (John Wiley, New York). Actually, the book was published in 1973, and the term and technique were introduced by Pyhrr, a management consultant, in an article in *Harvard Business Review* for November-December, 1970. Fortunately for the author, Mr. Carter read that article, and, in 1971 when he was governor of Georgia, he hired the consultant to install the system in that state. As of this writing, estimates of ongoing installations vary from 30 to 100, including states and cities and a number of companies in the private sector.

One commercial user reporting pronounced success with the system is Florida Power & Light Company. In March of 1977, the process was adopted for all FPL General Office staff departments. The essence of the program as reported by the company's director of Management Control, Ben Dady, is that managers start with "zero" budget dollars each year, then prove the case—activity by activity or project by project—for all the dollars they propose to spend. New and existing problems are placed on an equal footing, since both are being rated according to their relative effectiveness. Each manager or supervisor activity is thoroughly identified and then evaluated by considering (1) better alternative ways, and (2) different levels of performing that same function. Then a ranking plan establishes relative priorities.

While much of the publicity attending zero-base budgeting has given the impression that it is a revolutionary new technique, that is not the case. The process has many similarities to PPBS (Planning-Programming-Budgeting System), introduced in many governmental agencies and jurisdictions in the 1960s. Both concepts involve analyzing the inputs and outputs for specific programs, rather than relying exclusively on the traditional line-item format.

As described by Pyhrr, the philosophy and procedures used to install zero-base budgeting in industry and government are almost identical, with the mechanics differing slightly to fit the needs of each user. The process requires each manager to justify his entire budget request in detail, and puts the burden of proof on him to justify why he should spend *any* money.

Each manager must prepare a "decision package" for each activity or operation, and this package includes an analysis of cost, purpose, alternative courses of action, measures of performance, consequences of not performing the activity, and benefits. The analysis of alternatives as required by zero-base budgeting introduces a new concept to typical budgeting techniques. Managers must first identify different ways of performing each activity—such as centralizing versus decentralizing operations, or evaluating the economy of in house print shops versus commercial printers.

In addition, zero-base budgeting requires that managers identify different levels of effect for performing each activity. They must identify a minimum level of spending—often about 75% of their current operating level—and then identify in *separate* decision packages the costs and benefits of additional levels of spending for that activity. This analysis forces every manager to consider and evaluate a level of spending lower than his current operating level; gives management the alternative of eliminating an activity or choosing from several levels of effort; and allows substantial trade-offs and shifts in expenditure levels among organizational units.

Once the decision packages have been developed, they must be ranked or listed in order of importance. The ranking process allows each manager to identify his priorities explicitly, merges decision packages for ongoing and new programs into one ranking, and allows top management to evaluate and compare the relative needs and priorities of different organization units to make funding decisions.

ADVANTAGES

Advantages of zero-base budgeting as enumerated by Pyhrr are as follows: It provides top management with detailed information concerning the money needed to accomplish desired ends. It spotlights redundancies and duplication of effort among departments, focuses on dollars needed for programs rather than on the percentage increase or decrease from the previous year, specifies priorities within and among departments and divisions, allows comparisons across these organizational lines as to the respective priorities funded, and allows a performance audit to determine whether each activity or operation has performed as promised.

Changes in desired expenditure levels do not require the recycling of budget inputs, but the decision package ranking identifies those activities and operations (decision packages) to be added or deleted to produce the budget change. The list of ranking packages can also be used during the operating year to identify activities to be reduced or expanded if allowable expenditure levels change or actual costs vary from the budget. The process also gives top management a good tool with which to judge the performance of managers and employees, and gives managers a greater sense of responsibility for their budgets.

EVALUATION

A recent issue of *Harvard Business Review*[3] reports upon a thorough review of the burgeoning literature on zero-base budgeting, giving equal attention to the cons as well as the pros. The authors' review shows that many organizations have tried the technique in one form or another but found that it did not work. Properly implemented, however, zero-base budgeting can be a considerable improvement over the typical budgeting approach. It is noted that the number and nature of decision packages will vary from organization to organization. For example, the school district of Greece, N.Y., identified approximately 150 packages for the elementary, junior high, and senior high schools. The State of Georgia identified approximately 11,000 packages for its 1972–1973 fiscal year. It seems logical that any large organization can expect to have several thousand packages.

Setting priorites on the basis of the decision packages is not easy, since it is almost impossible for a group of executives in a large organization to have the expertise and the time to rank and establish priorities for thousands of packages. One solution, says the HBR article, is to have each manager rank his own packages, and then each senior executive rank the packages of all managers who report to him. This is the approach used by Texas Instruments, a

[3] "Where Does Zero-base Budgeting Work?" by James D. Suver and Ray L. Brown, respectively professors of accounting at the University of Colorado and the University of Denver, *Harvard Business Review*, November-December, 1977.

zero-base budgeting pioneer. Another approach is to let each level of management approve given amounts or percentages of those packages within its own area of responsibility. Thus the first level of review can rank and fund up to 50% of the proposed expenditures. The next level(s) may handle funding in the 50% to 80% range. Finally, top management only has to concentrate on the remaining part of the budget.

There appears to be general agreement that zero-base budgeting requires a lot of time, money, and paperwork. Developing decision packages takes a great deal of time. And a big problem is the review process. "Reviewing thousands of decision packages," says the HBR report, "is a monumental burden; reviewing them each year is a boring, not-too-productive Herculean task." The authors' final summation: "If you are dissatisfied with your present budgeting system, or are uneasy about the magnitude of some of your administrative programs, you will find that zero-base budgeting provides you with a systematic method of addressing your problems . . . It requires training, lots of time, lots of paperwork and measurements that enable every decision package to be ranked. . . . There is good and bad in zero-base budgeting."

11
Direct (Variable) Costing

Direct Costing[1] is a practical accounting technique for implementing the economic theory of marginal analysis to guide the making of short-run business decisions. Underlying direct costing is the classification of costs recorded in the accounts and reported in the income statement into (a) *direct* or *variable* costs which tend to vary directly and proportionately with the current rate of activity, and (b) *period* or *fixed* costs which tend to persist unchanged in total amount within the usual range of activity fluctuations. The direct costing income statement characteristically displays relationships between costs, sales volume, and profits for the period covered by the statement. Knowing these relationships, costs, and profit margins can be readily projected for other volumes within the range for which cost-volume relationships remain stable.

In *absorption costing*, which is the alternative to direct costing, no distinction is made between direct (or variable) and period (or fixed) costs in the accounts and income statement. Production is costed at rates including a proportionate share of period manufacturing costs, a characteristic which has given rise to the term absorption costing. Where absorption costing is in effect, resort

[1] As noted in Chapter 5, direct costing is also commonly referred to in the literature as "variable" costing.

must be had to supplementary statistical analysis to disclose relationships between costs, volume, and profits.

Direct costing is not a complete cost accounting method, but rather is a feature introduced into standard or actual process or job order cost systems to make them more useful. Neither is it a revision to primitive costing methods which determined only prime manufacturing cost of products, for direct costing implies analysis and classification of all costs (including selling and administrative costs) into direct and period components. Users of direct costing do allocate period costs to products for purposes such as pricing, but these allocations are made statistically and by methods flexible with the purpose instead of routinely in the accounts. In practice, many cost systems combine features of both direct and absorption costing.

HISTORICAL BACKGROUND

Early cost accountants attempted to stabilize unit costs under conditions of fluctuating volume by charging production with overhead rates predicated on a so-called normal or standard volume. Since volume cannot be controlled to a standard level, under or overabsorbed cost balances arise in the accounts. These volume variances enter into the reckoning of periodic profit or loss, but they are not easily associated with the specific increments in output or sales which are the subject of many management decisions. Moreover, the practice of absorbing fixed costs in inventory causes reported profit or loss to be influenced by changes in the inventory of manufactured goods even when sales and other factors remain constant. As a consequence, using absorption costing, increased sales may be accompanied by lower profit if the inventory is reduced in the same period. Conversely, reported profit can be increased by producing goods for inventory in the face of declining sales.

Relationships between net profit determined by the direct costing method and by the absorption costing method are illustrated by Exhibit I. In this illustration, changes in profits from period to period are attributable solely to changes in volume of sales and production, because other factors which would affect profits are assumed to be constant.

It is seen that sales in the second quarter are lower than in the first quarter, but the absorption costing method shows an increase in net profit. The situation is reversed in the third quarter when, despite a sales volume larger than that in either of the preceding periods, the profit reported by absorption costing is lower than in the preceding periods. Sales volume is identical in the third and fourth quarters, but profit reported by absorption costing differs. On the other hand, it can be seen that profits have a consistent relationship to sales volume when direct costing is used. When sales and production are in balance (as in the first quarter and for the year as a whole), profits reported by the two methods are identical. Differences between profits reported by the two methods are explained by the amount of fixed cost deferred in inventory by absorption costing, as shown by the reconciliation at the bottom of Exhibit I.

Absorption costing tends to accentuate profit fluctuations in companies which experience cyclical swings in sales and profits because these companies usually increase inventories of manufactured products during periods of rising activity and reduce inventories during periods of recession. Growing companies find that a portion of current fixed cost is capitalized indefinitely because larger inventories are needed to support an expanded volume of sales. As a result, periodic profits tend to be over-stated. Under direct costing, decisions to increase or decrease inventory of manufactured goods do not affect profits.

The development of direct costing was motivated by the desire to have incremental cost and profit data to guide decisions and by the desire to clarify the income statement in order that management might better understand the interaction of volume, costs, and profits. An N.A.A. research study ("Direct Costing," *Research Report No. 23*) showed that early applications of direct costing were made independently in a number of different companies. A second N.A.A. research study, conducted to ascertain how direct costing is being used, summarized the experience of fifty companies ("Current Applications of Direct Costing," *Research Report*

EXHIBIT I

COMPARISON BETWEEN ABSORPTION COSTING AND DIRECT COSTING METHODS

Quarterly Budget (In absorption costing form with fixed and variable costs separated)

	Total	Per Unit
Sales (30,000 units)	$30,000	$1.00
Cost of Goods Sold		
Variable Costs	19,500	.65
Fixed Costs	6,000	.20
Total	25,500	.85
Gross Margin	4,500	.15
Selling and Administrative Costs (fixed)	2,100	.07
Operating profit	$ 2,400	.08

Actual Production and Sales in Units

	1st Quarter	2nd Quarter	3rd Quarter	4th Quarter	Year
Opening Inventory	—	—	6,000	2,000	—
Production	30,000	34,000	28,000	30,000	122,000
Sales	30,000	28,000	32,000	32,000	122,000
Closing Inventory	—	6,000	2,000	—	—

Income Statement by Quarters and for Year

1. Using *Absorption Costing* with Fixed Manufacturing Cost Charged to Production at Predetermined Overhead Rate of $0.20 per Unit Based on Budgeted Volume and Budgeted Overhead Cost.

	Quarters				Year
	1	2	3	4	
Sales	$30,000	$28,000	$32,000	$32,000	$122,000
Cost of Goods Manufactured	25,500	28,900	23,800	25,500	103,700
Add Opening Inventory	—	—	5,100	1,700	
Cost of Goods Available	25,500	28,900	28,900	27,200	
Deduct Closing Inventory	—	5,100	1,700	—	
Cost of Goods Sold	25,500	23,800	27,200	27,200	103,700
Under or (Over) Absorbed Overhead	—	(800)	400	—	(400)
Total	25,500	23,000	27,600	27,200	103,300
Gross Margin	4,500	5,000	4,400	4,800	18,700
Selling and Administrative Costs	2,100	2,100	2,100	2,100	8,400
Net Operating Profit	$ 2,400	$ 2,900	$ 2,300	$ 2,700	$ 10,300

(continued on following page)

EXHIBIT I (*Continued*)

2. Using *Direct Costing* with Fixed Manufacturing Costs Treated as Period Costs.

	1	2	3	4	Year
Sales	$30,000	$28,000	$32,000	$32,000	$122,000
Cost of Goods Manufactured	19,500	22,100	18,200	19,500	79,300
Add Opening Inventory	—	—	3,900	1,300	
Cost of Goods Available	19,500	22,100	22,100	20,800	
Deduct Closing Inventory	—	3,900	1,300	—	
Cost of Goods Sold	19,500	18,200	20,800	20,800	79,300
Marginal Income	10,500	9,800	11,200	11,200	42,700
Fixed Costs					
Manufacturing	6,000	6,000	6,000	6,000	24,000
Selling and Administrative	2,100	2,100	2,100	2,100	8,400
Total	8,100	8,100	8,100	8,100	32,400
Net Operating Profit	$ 2,400	$ 1,700	$ 3,100	$ 3,100	$ 10,300

Reconciliation of Differences in Reported Profits

	Quarters				Year
	1	2	3	4	
Absorption Cost Profit	$2,400	$2,900	$2,300	$2,700	$10,300
Direct Cost Profit	2,400	1,700	3,100	3,100	10,300
Difference	$ —	$1,200	$(800)	$(400)	—
Change in Inventory (in units)	—	6,000	(4,000)	(2,000)	—
Change in Amount of Fixed Cost in Inventory*	—	$1,200	$(800)	$(400)	—

*Calculated by multiplying change in number of units by $0.20.
SOURCE: "Direct Costing," N.A.A. *Research Report 23.* 1953.

No. 37). Since publication of the foregoing N.A.A. study, interest in direct costing has grown rapidly, and applications now exist in many companies. However, for reasons stated subsequently, applications of direct costing are, with a few exceptions, limited to internal records and reports.

The term *marginal costing* generally replaces direct costing in British accounting terminology.

THEORY OF DIRECT COSTING

Under direct costing, determination of income proceeds by first deducting from sales revenues all of the direct costs of making and selling goods represented by sales revenues of the period. The resulting difference, termed *marginal income* or *contribution margin*, measures the amount contributed by the period's sales toward period costs and profit. Inventory is costed at direct cost because only these costs are causally associated with inventory in the sense that they were incurred specifically because the goods were produced in the current period and, to the extent that goods are carried forward in inventory, the same costs will be avoided in the future.

In a second step, period costs are deducted from marginal income to arrive at net profit. Period costs arise from provision of capacity to make and sell in the form of facilities and organization which remain relatively constant through ordinary fluctuations in production and sales. The full amount of period cost recognized in each period is deducted from income of the same period because the opportunity to use this capacity tends to expire with time whether or not it is fully utilized.

An illustration appears in Exhibit II. It may be noted that period costs specific to the product are shown separately because these period costs would be eliminated if the product were dropped. In practice, repetitive allocations of common period costs may be omitted because these allocations are unavoidably subjective and unreliable.

SCOPE OF DIRECT COSTING

Attention is called to the following characteristics of the direct costing income statement.

Exhibit II

Product Line Income Statement Using Direct Costing

	Total		Product Lines No. 1		No. 2		No. 3	
	Amount	Pct.	Amount	Pct.	Amount	Pct.	Amount	Pct
Net Sales	$600,000	100.0	$300,000	100.0	$200,000	100.0	$100,000	100.0
Direct Costs								
Manufacturing								
Direct Materials	$150,000	25.0	$ 75,000	25.0	$ 55,000	27.5	$ 20,000	20.0
Direct Labor	90,000	15.0	30,000	10.0	30,000	15.0	30,000	30.0
Direct Overhead	60,000	10.0	30,000	10.0	20,000	10.0	10,000	10.0
Selling								
Freight Out	12,000	2.0	9,000	3.0	3,000	1.5	—	—
Salesmen's Commissions	24,000	4.0	12,000	4.0	8,000	4.0	4,000	4.0
Total Direct Costs	$336,000	56.0	$156,000	52.0	$116,000	58.0	$ 64,000	64.0
Marginal Income	$264,000	44.0	$144,000	48.0	$ 84,000	42.0	$ 36,000	36.0

Period Costs Specific to Product Lines							
Depreciation	$ 40,000		$ 20,000		$ 10,000		$ 10,000	
Property Taxes and Insurance	20,000		10,000		2,000		8,000	
Advertising	24,000		20,000		—		4,000	
Total	$ 84,000		$ 50,000		$ 12,000		$ 22,000	
Margin after specific period costs	$180,000	30.0	$ 94,000	31.3	$ 72,000	36.0	14,000	14.0
Allocated General Period Costs							
Manufacturing	$ 40,000		$ 20,000		$ 13,320		$ 6,680	
Selling	30,000		15,000		10,000		5,000	
Administrative	30,000		15,000		10,000		5,000	
Research & Development	20,000		10,000		6,666		3,334	
Total	$120,000		$ 60,000		$ 39,986		$ 20,014	
Profit (loss) before taxes	$ 60,000	10.0	$ 34,000	10.3	$ 32,014	16.5	($ 6,014)	(6.0)

SOURCE: "Current Application of Direct Costing," *N.A.A. Research Report No. 37.*

(1) Total marginal income varies directly and proportionately with sales within the range for which period costs remain constant. Hence unit marginal income can be used to project the contribution to profit from increments in sales and to evaluate *relative* profitability of products and other segments of the business.

(2) Significant figures such as sales volume required to break even or to earn a target rate of return on capital employed, selling price required to break even or to earn a target rate of return from a given volume, and effect on profits of changes in direct and period costs are readily estimated from data appearing in the income statement itself.

(3) Net profit varies with sales and is not affected by buildup or liquidation of inventory.

The foregoing characteristics make direct costing particularly useful in profit planning, budgeting, and pricing. The same characteristics facilitate analysis and explanation of reported operating results because they bring accounting for past events into conformity with patterns of thinking which management follows in planning for the future. Rapid spread in internal application of direct costing is attributable to its uses for these purposes.

Direct costing also has usefulness in controlling current costs, although it is not primarily a tool for cost control. This usefulness stems from the fact that knowledge of how individual cost items should respond to changes in volume is helpful to managers responsible for controlling these costs. An additional advantage may be gained from having the amounts of period costs collected and reported in the income statement instead of having these costs lost to sight by allocation between cost of sales and inventory.

Applications of direct costing are usually confined to internal reports prepared for management use, although there is no theoretical reason why some of the same advantages gained by management should not extend to outside shareholders and creditors. However, the use of direct costing in external financial reports has often been opposed by certified public accountants because it represents a change from established conventions in external reporting. Direct costing has not been accepted for determining taxable income, presumably because losses of tax revenue would result from write-off period costs in inventories in the change-over period and subsequently from current deduction of period costs which would otherwise be deferred as a business grows and its inventories increase.

For these reasons, external financial reports are usually prepared on the conventional absorption costing basis. The difference between profit determined by the two methods is explained by the change in the amount of period costs deferred in inventory. Where cost accounts are on a direct costing basis, an adjusting figure can be computed by relatively simple procedures at the end of each period to convert inventory and cost of goods sold to an absorption costing basis. Adjustments are applied to summary figures only and not to component details which appear in the internal records and reports.

12

Statistical Accounting

Statistical accounting denotes the application of probability theory and statistical sampling techniques to the general area of accounting. Clerical acounting operations have become a costly activity in many businesses because of the large masses of data which must be processed. Statistical accounting techniques provide a means of reducing such costs significantly by developing the necessary accounting information through projections of results obtained from processing only selected samples of the basic accounting data, while still providing the required degree of reliability with a known degree of risk. In appropriate applications, with proper planning, the results achieved may be as reliable, if not more so, as those obtained through other means.

FORMAL DEFINITION

Statistical accounting is the application of the concepts of probability theory and the techniques of statistical sampling to the development of prime accounting data and/or the verification, authentication, and audit of accounting data prepared by other means.

HISTORY

The use of statistical sampling and probability theory in business obtained its major impetus in the area of production quality control during World War II. Subsequent thereto, the same concepts and techniques were applied to quality control of clerical operations and gradually extended during the late 1950s to include the development of prime accounting data. During this same period, the techniques also began to receive increasing attention in connection with internal and independent public auditing procedures.

APPROACHES AND TECHNIQUES

The applications of statistical accounting may be classified into two groups. The first involves the development of prime accounting data. One of the earliest and most widely publicized applications involves the taking of physical inventories. Using statistical sampling, only selected items (perhaps less than 10% of the total number of items) are counted, priced, and extended. The results are projected to obtain the value for the total inventory. Results obtained are frequently within 1% or 2% tolerance limits, with 95% or greater reliability. A comparable degree of error may exist in a 100% physical inventory taken at considerably greater cost. Other examples of applications in use today are the interline settlement of ticket revenues between various airlines, the aging of accounts receivable, the establishment of warranty reserves, and the development of price indices for LIFO ("last in, first out") inventory valuations. In each of these cases, the dollar amounts of business transactions and accounting entries are based on a projection of results obtained from a statistical sample of the total data.

The second area of application is in the verification, authentication, and audit of accounting data originally compiled by some other means. Typical accounting applications involve the verification of vendors' invoices before payment, the rechecking of payroll computations, and the checking of customer billings. In each case, the statistical approach is used in lieu of 100% checking to establish the degree of error existing in the data. If an unsatisfactory condition is detected, special corrective action, including perhaps a complete reprocessing of the data, can be undertaken. Internal and independent internal auditors have also begun to use statistical techniques in order to ensure that their audit tests provide the desired degree of assurance. When audit tests are made using statistical sampling techniques, the degree of reliability and precision of the results can be evaluated mathematically. When such tests are made solely on the basis of judgment sampling, their reliability cannot be evaluated objectively. Typical audit applications include the confirmation of accounts receivable and payable, the vouching of cash receipts and disbursements, and the checking of inventory pricings.

The successful application of statistical accounting techniques requires a fairly sophisticated analysis of the problem area, the objectives to be obtained, and the characteristics of the accounting data involved. After business management has established risk and reliability tolerances, trained statisticians can prepare working plans for sample size, selection, and analysis, based on mathematical formulae, to obtain the desired results. The results obtained may be subjected to further statistical tests to assure that the desired degree of reliability and risk have been obtained.

ACCEPTANCE

While there is considerable difference of opinion as to the extent to which statistical accounting will ultimately be applied, such differences do not involve the basic soundness of the approach. Many large companies that have utilized the techniques on a limited experimental basis, such as General Electric Company, Gulf Oil Co., and Minneapolis-Honeywell Co., have found the results very satisfactory and are extending their applications. In the area of auditing, various public accounting firms, internal audit staffs, and governmental audit agencies have found many useful applications.

The techniques have not yet been adopted as standard auditing procedures by the American Institute of Certified Public Accountants, though their use has been recognized as being in conformance with generally accepted auditing standards. Certain unresolved problems inherent in the nature of auditing tests remain. However, auditors who have used statistical techniques believe their results to date warrant continued expansion in their use.

13
Marketing Cost Analysis

Marketing cost analysis in its broadest sense is concerned with the study of the costs incurred from the time goods are manufactured to final delivery and payment, with a view toward providing the members of the marketing organization with useful quantitative financial information. The information is designed to aid in planning, decision making, and control at all levels of the marketing organization. The tools of analyses employed are derived from accounting and other related disciplines using quantitative methods.

It should be pointed out that the term *marketing* as used here is more than selling or order getting. It includes the activities of personal selling (field selling), impersonal selling (advertising, sales promotion, etc.), physical distribution (warehousing, order filling, and shipping), marketing research, and any other function assigned to a marketing department. The definition is particularly relevant in the light of the wide adoption of what is called the *marketing concept*. Progressive companies have accepted a changed view of the marketing function. Its task is no longer viewed as selling that which has been produced. Instead, marketing is placed at "the beginning" of the process. It is the function of marketing to ascertain market needs, present and future, as guides to research. By its forecast, marketing indicates what will be sold, when, to whom, and at what price. Manufacturing as well as research are then geared to the market needs. This has resulted in new and important responsibilities for the marketing executive. As an important member of the management team, he must be concerned with more than just sales volume. He is now concerned, as are his colleagues on the top management team, with maximizing the return on the investment in the business through effective planning, decision making, and control.

MARKETING COST INFORMATION

Defining Needs.   In developing financial information for marketing management, the analyst must have a clear understanding of the specific responsibilities assigned to the members of the marketing management team. This provides knowledge on the types of problems faced, the kinds of information necessary in planning and decision making, and on the control areas delegated. This is most important because of the inclination of accounting-oriented analysts to design information based on a limited perception of the marketing operation, resulting in reports and analyses which fail to meet the needs of marketing managers and as a result are rarely used. It has frequently been observed that the critical problem in marketing cost analysis is the difficulty of communication between financial executives and marketing people because of the limited perception of problems and capabilities.

Among others, information needs of marketing managers relate to problems of:

(1) Product mix (the quantities of the different products to be sold).

(2) Product addition or deletion.

(3) Marketing mix (the extent of utilization of different strategies—advertising, promotion, personal selling, etc.

(4) Salesman (performance, goals and evaluation, compensation plans).

(5) Customer volume or order size (the problem of the small order).

(6) Prices.

It is well to stress that marketing cost analysis stresses *profits* rather than mere *sales volume* as a goal, and is one of the indications of the transition from mere "selling" to marketing. In addition, costs are classified by marketing functions, and since functions are the responsibility of people, it leads to the adoption of responsibility reporting. (See Section II, RESPONSIBILITY REPORTING, in Chapter 10, BUDGETING.) Budgets and standards can thus be used for evaluating performance.

FUNCTIONAL CLASSIFICATION

The analyst abstracts raw data from accounting records, the latter oriented toward financial reporting for the entire enterprise. Accordingly, the costs of marketing operations are listed in so-called *natural classifications*, wherein the object of the expenditure (salaries, supplies, depreciation, insurance) is employed and is relevant for financial and tax reporting. However, for marketing cost analysis, these expenses have to be recast in terms of the functions performed by marketing. This means the assignment of portions of natural expenses to activities of the marketing organization as related to the delegation of authority therein. The two types of classification are illustrated in Exhibit I.

The determination of functional costs serves to associate costs with responsibilities and also provides the basis for assigning costs to segments of the marketing operation. Accordingly, costs may be assigned to product or product groups, to customers and groups of customers as channels of distribution, to geographic units of the full marketing organization (territories, districts, regions), to groups of orders by size of order, etc. Practices in assigning costs vary as is evidenced by the summary of the practices of twenty-eight large companies in Exhibit II. A useful test for the assignment of cost to segments is *causation*, which requires that the factor controlling the occurrence of a cost and its variation be the basis used.

PRODUCT AND CUSTOMER COSTS

An alternate approach suggests the classification of marketing functions into three groups: product costs; customer costs; and other costs. *Product costs* are those costs which are related to

EXHIBIT I

A COMPARISON OF NATURAL AND FUNCTIONAL EXPENSE STATEMENTS, 19—

Natural Expense Statement		Functional Expense Statement		
Salaries and wages	$272,996	Sales		
Truck expenses	53,498	Floor selling	$ 937	
Traveling expense for salesmen	18,663	Telephone orders	644	
Depreciation—auto and trucks	8,618	Mail orders	2,119	
Depreciation — building and equipment	3,134	Outside selling	68,494	$ 72,194
Fuel and light	1,700	Office routines		
Repairs to building	7,542	Salesmen's ledgers	$ 1,642	
Rent	65	Commission calculations	487	2,129
Postage	1,938			
Stationery and office supplies	7,167	Advertising	$ 2,645	2,645
Insurance	19,833			
Telephone and telegraph	3,812	Credit		
Administrative car expense	398	Credit authorization	$ 8,664	
Advertising	2,071	Accounts receivable	10,619	19,283
Interest	9,936			
Pensions	2,400	Order routine		
Bad debts	4,039	Packing department forms	$ 4,870	
Taxes—state, county, and city	15,315	Pricing and extensions	6,575	

Taxes—federal old age, unemployment, excise	5,717	
Amortization of premium on U.S. bonds	1,799	
General expenses—legal, auditing, and contributions	7,654	
Invoice typing	9,435	
Cashier	3,009	23,889
Buying		
Buying	$ 6,208	
Accounts payable	707	
Receiving	15,583	22,498
Storage	$ 35,750	35,750
Stamping	$ 2,899	2,899
Order filling		
Packing	$ 16,314	
Shipping	62,166	
Checking	5,039	
Loading	13,474	96,993
Delivery		
Routing	$ 2,619	
Delivery	124,815	127,434
Executive and general	$ 42,581	42,581
Total	$448,295	$448,295

(From Longman and Schiff, "Practical Distribution Cost Analyses.")

EXHIBIT II

BASES OF ALLOCATION OF JOINT COSTS
(Summary of bases used by 28 companies)

Function	Products	Customer Classes	Territories
Advertising	Standard cost of goods sold.	Direct to products; to customers in terms of purchases.	Circulation by area. Direct to products, then to districts on units sold.
Promotion		Direct to products; to customers in terms of purchases.	
Personal Selling	Budget unit volume. Planned effort. Estimated time. Direct to dealer on time basis, then to products. Commissions, direct. Time log, test basis.	Estimated time, salary expense. Commissions direct.	Cases shipped.
Storage	Pallet units. Av. inventory vol. No. of invoice lines. Space reserved. Costs for storing specific products. Taxes, value of average inventory. Fixed costs, space used.	Allocated to products, then to customers on products purchased.	Allocated to product groups, then to districts on units shipped.

Order-Filling, Physical	Estimated time of warehousemen. Number of cases. Gallons handled. Standard handling units. No. of invoice lines. Performance standards for functions.	Allocated to products, then to customers on products purchased. Average cost per unit times billings.		Same as storage.
Delivery	Analysis of freight bills. Freight rates times product. Freight factor times weight. Mileage times rate per mile, by type of vehicle. Time times rate per time, and driver reports. Fixed costs—stops, stop time, miles. Variable costs—miles.	Same as product.	Same as product.	Average facility charge for fixed vehicle costs; other costs direct.
Order-Filling, Clerical—Sales Accounting	Budgeted units. Number of invoice lines. Cost per line for various forms. Number of invoices and average volume per invoice. Some direct, others cost per invoice times number of invoices.	Cost per line for various forms. Number of invoices and average volume per invoice.		Number of invoice lines.

(continued on following page.)

EXHIBIT II —*Continued*

Function	Products	Consumer Classes	Territories
General and Administrative	Budgeted unit volume. Based on all other costs. Estimated effort. Projected sales dollars. Shipments. Production, assets, manpower. Detailed functionalization and multibases.	Based on all other costs.	
Product Management	Standard cost of goods. Estimated time.	Direct to products, then in terms of products purchased.	Direct to products, then to districts on sales dollars.
Research	Projects, direct. Basic, standard cost of goods sold as based on direct.		Direct to product groups, then to districts on sales dollars.
Credit	Allocated to class of customers, distribution to product groups on sales dollars of products.	Same as products.	To customers, then to territories in which located.

SOURCE: Schiff and Hellman, "Financial Management of the Marketing Function."

Exhibit III
Marketing Cost and Bases of Allocation

Functional Cost Group	Total	Basis of Allocation
Customer Costs		

Functional Cost Group	Total	Basis of Allocation
Outside Selling		
Personnel cost (commissions, etc.)	$254,820	Dollar Sales
Travel and auto costs	114,040	Call—Miles
Sales supervision	104,814	Calls
Sales Call Reports		
Sales Records (order review, traffic, postage and stationery for invoices)	61,458	Orders
Accounts Receivable Posting		
Invoice Typing (personnel costs, etc.)	19,556	Orders × 3 plus invoice lines
Credit Authorization		
Credit manager, etc.	15,614	Per customer
Bad debts	36,000	Direct
Collection	1,120	Direct
Accounts Receivable— Interest on borrowed funds	22,500	Average Balance
	$629,922	

Product Costs		
Advertising	$357,448	Direct
Finished Goods Storage		
(Interest on borrowed funds)	40,500	Average inventory value
(Space costs)	30,932	Space—sq. ft.
Packing—(supplies)	64,000	Direct
Packing, Trucking, Supervision	119,480	No. of units sold × handling unit
	$612,360	

Executive and General		
General Selling, Accounting, Executive, etc.	$314,048	

Derived from Longman and Schiff, *Practical Distribution Cost Analysis*, R. D. Irwin, 1955.

EXHIBIT IV

MARGINAL CONTRIBUTION ON SALES
OF A PRODUCT

Net Sales		$2,100,000	100.00%
Cost of Goods Sold		1,702,800	81.09
Gross Profit		$ 397,200	18.91%
Product Costs:			
Inventory Car-rying Costs	$ 10,733		
Inventory Space Costs	7,284		
Handling Costs	28,974		
Product Adver-tising	104,320		
Packing Sup-plies	19,000	170,311	8.11
Marginal Contribu-tion for Customer Costs, General Administrative Overhead, and Profit		$ 226,889	10.80%

products—their physical characteristics and related marketing activities. *Customer costs* are those which depend upon where the customer is located, how he buys, and when he buys. The rest of the costs not governed by either products or customers are classified as *other costs.*

A classification of marketing costs on this basis appears in Exhibit III, which also includes the bases used in allocating these costs to specific products and customer groups. This approach permits the preparation of reports showing the profit contribution by product before allocation of customer costs, and conversely the profit contribution by customer before allocation of product costs. It therefore follows closely the delegation of responsibility within the marketing organization. A product manager's report should focus on profit contribution after product costs—those costs which he can influence (Exhibit IV). Similarly, the manager of sales to a channel of distribution (department stores, chain stores, supermarkets, etc.) should receive a report which shows profit contribution after those customer costs which he can influence (Exhibit V).

Variations in reporting financial information to marketing

EXHIBIT V
MARGINAL CONTRIBUTION ON SALES IN A
CHANNEL OF DISTRIBUTION

Net Sales			$160,000	100.00%
Cost of Goods Sold			121,200	75.75
Gross Profit			$ 38,800	24.25%
Customer Costs:				
Sales Salaries and Commissions	$ 5,096			
Traveling	18,535			
Invoice Typing and Sales Records	3,103			
Accounts Receivable Records	652			
Credit Authorization	780			
Collection	140			
Bad Debts	7,000		35,306	22.07
Marginal Contribution for Product Costs, General Administrative Overhead, and Profit			$ 3,494	2.18%

management occur in different firms because of differences in the market faced, strategies and tactics employed, and the organization of the marketing effort. A portion of a list of reports reviewed in a field study of practices in a number of large companies is shown in Exhibit VI.

FULL COSTING v. MARGINAL COSTING

Apart from the problem of defining responsibilities and designing information about responsibilities, there is continuing difference of opinion among analysts on the desirability of reallocating fixed costs to segments of the marketing department. It is maintained by one group that no fixed costs should be allocated, because they are not relevant in evaluating specific product or market performance. The opposing group urges that failure to incorporate fixed costs ignores the availability of services reflected in fixed costs which may be shifted from less profitable to more profitable uses.

It is submitted here that most of the controversy stems from a failure to delineate clearly the objective for which an analysis is being made. Is it a product deletion or addition problem, a prob-

EXHIBIT VI

ACCOUNTING REPORTS FOR MARKETING

Control

1. Performance (control) reports giving (1) actual, (2) variance from budget (predetermined standard of performance), and (3) ratio of variance to budget (year-to-date and for month) for each:
   a. Salesman (sales and cost to gross profit).
   b. Sales district manager (sales, cost and expense to district operating profit).
   c. Product group (sales, cost and expense to gross profit or profit contribution).
   d. Division or department (sales, cost and expense to division operating profit).
2. Supervision of salesmen (areas for improvement):
3. For any product, group of products or profit-investment center, the trend of merchandising profit and ratios to sales and investment over a period of years. (In this case investment includes cost of establishing territory [district or region] as well as allocation of working capital and manufacturing facilities.)
4. Sales vs. potential, trend for five-year period.
5. Customer analysis, by customer:
   a. Annual sales and total profit contribution.
   b. Annual sales and gross profit by products.
   c. Number and average size of orders.
   d. Payment and credit received.
   e. Reciprocity record.
6. Listing of customers (within districts) by:
   a. Type of selling or frequency of salesmen's calls.
   b. Importance (volume) for reciprocity purposes.
   c. Credit ratings.
7. Production vs. capacity.

Order Processing and Billing

1. Standard costs of order processing and billing:
   a. Per unit product,
   b. Variations due to complexity of orders, number of items, back ordering, and items on invoice.

Physical Distribution

1. Comparison of:
   a. Profit from shipments direct from plant, with
   b. Profit from shipments through a regional or district warehouse.
2. Studies of shipments from several plants to various markets considering variable costs.

Physical Order Filling

1. Receiving, handling, shipping: standard costs per unit of shipment.
2. Packing: standard costs per unit of shipment.
3. Other costs:
   a. Those variable with "in" and "out" activity
   b. Those variable with inventory size.
   c. Those variable with other specific factors.
   d. Fixed or Period costs.

EXHIBIT VI—*Continued*

4. Economic analysis of alternative packaging.
5. Economic analysis of alternative delivery methods including packing for shipment, shipping, transportation, and delivery.
6. Analysis of alternative warehousing plans.

Product Pricing

1. Variable costs, whole costs, variable (marginal) profit, gross profit, gross profit and merchandising profit per unit of each product.
2. Analysis of price elasticity of various products (response of change in sales to change in price); and change in net profit resulting from a change (up or down) in price of product.

Profitability Reports

1. Reports of product cost and profit:
   a. Variable cost (within specific production capacity): (1) pricing, short term; (2) to determine contribution to pool; (3) to secure costs quickly without allocating overhead; (4) buy or make decisions (short run); (5) allocation of production to plants.
   b. Whole cost (within specified production capacity): (1) long-range relative profitability; (2) long-range pricing; (3) long-range study of business; (4) long-range budgeting.

Salesmen's Compensation and Performance

1. For each salesman, for year:
   a. Sales and gross margin (or gross profit if variable costs to secure gross margin are not available for each salesman).
   b. Total compensation and ratio: (1) to sales; and, (2) to gross margin (or gross profit).
2. Studies to indicate increasing productivity of salesmen with experience (years of service).
3. Cost of turnover of salesmen:
4. Appraisal of performance (actual sales compared to potential, or after measure) with compensation paid.
5. Comparison of selling time to travel time.
6. Analysis of costs of alternative methods of providing transportation for salesmen.
7. Reports of performance of salesmen compared to specific budget items.
8. Reports for control of salesmen include:
   a. Sales volume vs. sales quotas and potential.
   b. Calls per day by class of customer.
   c. Number and average size of orders.
   d. Orders per call.
   e. Direct selling expense per call.
   f. Direct selling expense per order.
   g. Sales coverage, ratio of desired number of customers to total prospects in territory.
   h. Call frequency ratio.
9. Analysis of salesmen's compensation plans, considering whether they:
   a. Provide an incentive.
   b. Minimize the effect of windfalls and compensate when adverse conditions prevail.

EXHIBIT VI—*Continued*
    c. Reward or penalize the salesman only for factors over which he has control.
    d. Are easily understood, interpreted, and administered.
    e. Compensate for qualitative as well as quantitative results.
    f. Base incentive on volume, product or customer mix, or profit.
    g. Compensate for differences in territorial potential and competition.
    h. Place a ceiling on total earnings.
    i. Result in a maximization of the firm's return on its investment in the territory.
    j. Facilitate budgeting.

Size of Orders

1. Determine for each unit of product intrinsic* "delivered" costs which vary with:
    a. Number of orders.
    b. Value of orders.
    c. Number of items per order.
    d. Number of invoice lines.
    e. Any other significant variable factors, or,
    f. Are unrelated to above factors (fixed).
2. Based on above costs, determine for each unit of product:
    a. "Delivered" cost, and
    b. Profit contribution (sales less "delivered cost") for various sizes of orders.

Special Studies

1. Analysis of profit with alternative patterns or channels of distribution, or with alternative choices of product mix or marketing mix.
2. Estimate of net added profit from additions to product line, after allowing for loss of profit due to decreases in volume of existing products as a result of selling the new line; also, return on added investment.
3. Estimate of difference in net profit between selling direct and selling through distributors, jobbers, or agents.
4. Estimate of minimum added sales required to provide sufficient earnings to offset cost of the following:
    a. Special services to customers.
    b. Product advertising.
    c. Sales promotion.
    d. A price cut of X per cent.
5. Analyses of trend of share of the market.
6. Evaluation of benefits from selling products with warranty vs. cost of warranty.

*Intrinsic delivered costs include product costs, packing and shipping, selling expense, order handling, billing, and transportation to customer (unless sold F.O.B. plant).
SOURCE: Schiff and Mellman, "Financial Management of the Marketing Function."

lem involving shifting of advertising effort, one of adding or deleting a territory, or a problem of alternate methods of delivery? Herein the relevant costs, fixed or variable, *those affected by the decision*, are the only ones to be considered. On the other hand, the evaluation of performance should relate the revenue and costs affected by a given level of management and the assets risked in the case of a revenue producing activity. Where revenue is not produced, then costs which are controllable should be related to activity and measured by output.

The change in marketing management's attitude toward profits and maximization of return on investment is reflective of the new responsibilities assigned. Profit *responsibility* is readily replacing profit *awareness*, and the tendency to deal with segments of the marketing organization as profit centers results in both a need for adequate financial information, as well as an understanding of the financial implications of decisions made. This is true of the vice president of marketing developing a long- or short-term marketing plan, as well as of the salesman developing his approach in meeting a customer or a prospect. It also suggests the need for integrating financial information with information developed by marketing research and operations research. For example, an increase in sales *and* profits of a given product group beyond plan may be reported, but when associated with share of market information it may show a decline because of an increase in total market potential. Similarly, a decrease in warehousing cost below budgeted levels might not reflect increased efficiency if a study of operations reveals either poorer service rendered, or perhaps a more effective way of providing warehousing service then the one in use which would result in improved service at a lower cost.

The challenge for additional effort and study in developing better coordinated information for marketing management is underscored by the huge expenditures for marketing functions. Here is a fertile area for creative work which will yield a sizeable return on the effort invested.

14

Industrial Research Accounting

Since research and development operations are largely non-repetitive and the end result is usable knowledge rather than a tangible product, techniques applied in industrial research accounting differ somewhat from those commonly applied to manufacturing operations.

DEFINITION OF FUNCTION

Specific definitions differ from company to company because the nature of the activities carried on and the manner in which they are organized differ. As stated in the National Association of Accountants *NAA Research Report No. 29:*

> Research and development comprises a variety of activities, including search for new products and new manufacturing processes; improvement of existing products, processes, and equipment; finding new uses for known products; solving technical problems arising in manufacture and application of products; and expanding general knowledge in basic scientific fields.

Some company organization plans assign to the research department responsibility for technical services applied to the elimination of manufacturing difficulties, routine testing of materials and products, and occasional production or sale of items requiring skills or equipment not available in the factory. While such functions are performed by research personnel, they are not necessarily looked upon as research activities. Consequently, costs of the work are often transferred to departments served. The research department in a small company usually performs a wider variety of tasks than it does in a large company where greater size permits more extensive subdivision of functions. The individual company's organization plan rather than some abstract definition of the research function usually governs in accounting for research costs.

A dividing line between Research and Production often needs to be established by company policy because there is overlapping at the stage where new products or methods developed by Research are being transferred to Production. This stage may include production with regular factory equipment, and work by research personnel to eliminate difficulties which arise in the early stages of production.

Good judgment applied to a specific organization generally yields a more useful definition of research than does application of a definition from some outside source.

CLASSIFYING RESEARCH COSTS

The plan of accounting realistically for research costs should provide classifications which permit desired reports to be prepared directly from the accounts. Provision should also be made for special analyses which may be desired from time to time.

NAA Research, No. 29 states that plans for classifying research costs are designed to provide answers to the following principal questions:

(1) How much was spent for research and development?

(2) Who spent it? (i.e., classification by responsibility for cost control).

(3) For what were the costs incurred? (i.e., classification by nature of expense).

(4) How was the effort of the research and development organization applied? (i.e., classification by project and division).

In order that cost may be accumulated under appropriate headings to answer such questions, accounts are set up and code numbers are assigned to them to facilitate data-processing operations.

One or more control accounts are needed to ascertain the total amount spent for research. Multiple control accounts are used when more than one major class of research cost is recognized. For example, one company uses the three control accounts listed below.

(1) *Control Account 15300—Research Expense*

Includes cost of operating the Research and Development Center, pilot plants operated by the Research and Development Center, the cost of services of outside laboratories, and expenses incurred by the staff of the Research and Development Center.

(2) *Control Account 15400—Research Development Expense*

Includes costs incurred in the development of the company for tests made at the request of the Research and Development Center.

(3) *Control Account 15600—Engineering Development Expense*

Includes costs incurred in the development and application of a new or redesigned machine or facility.

Major categories of research expense and the corresponding control accounts differ from company to company according to activities carried on and preferences of top management in each company.

RESPONSIBILITY FOR COST INCURRENCE

Accumulation of research costs by responsibilities for control is accomplished by use of a responsibility code. This code should follow the company's organization plan for its research activities. While the units in such a code may be divisions, departments, or other similar units, each should be an actual organization unit headed by an individual in charge of activities within the unit. Otherwise, it is difficult or impossible to fix responsibility for costs.

Responsibility codes are illustrated in Exhibit I.

Research costs incurred are accumulated by accounts repre-

EXHIBIT I

TYPICAL RESPONSIBILITY CODES

Code Number	Unit Name	Supervisor	Location
6701	Plastic Research	C. Smith	Research center
6702	Ceramics Laboratory	E. Williams	Research center
6705	Motor Development Laboratory	O. Carlson	Chicago plant
6710	Project B Laboratory	E. Johnson	Cleveland
6713	Patent Department	J. Law	Research center
6714	Technical Library	A. Richards	Research center
6718	Research Administration	J. Keller	Research center

sented by numbers in the responsibility code. This permits cost reports showing by whom costs were incurred. Charges to each responsibility are best limited to items which the corresponding executive or supervisor is authorized to incur, for responsibility cannot be maintained for costs which the individual has no authority to control. If, for any reason, costs not controllable within a given responsibility are included in the charges, controllable and noncontrollable items should not be merged, but reported separately.

SOURCE OR ITEM OF EXPENSE

Within each responsibility, costs should be classified properly by source or item of expenditure. Research costs arise from the same basic sources (e.g., salaries and wages, supplies, occupancy of space, etc.) as do costs of other functions, and a uniform, company-wide classification is often used. This makes possible summarization of costs by source or item of expense for the company as a whole.

However, in some cases, it may be desirable to have additional expense source accounts to catalog expenses peculiar to research activities. Under decentralized management, a Research division is usually permitted to establish whatever accounts it considers helpful in guiding its operations. Accounts established should, however, be related to a general company chart of accounts so that accounts of the research division can be readily consolidated with those of other divisions.

APPLICATION OF RESEARCH EFFORT

Financial control over research activities is exercised primarily by controlling the application of effort and facilities to projects. A cumulative record of costs incurred as work progresses on each project is an essential aid in the process of financial control. The same record provides the basic information needed to allocate research cost to company divisions and to product lines benefited. If research is undertaken for customers or others outside the company, a knowledge of project cost is needed to ascertain profit or loss on each contract. A record of project cost is necessary for billing customers where research services are priced on a cost reimbursement basis.

Methods employed to determine costs of individual research projects are much like those used in job-order costing of manufacturing orders. Each research project is assigned a number and costs applied to the project are accumulated on a cost sheet or other suitable record.

When an extensive research program is carried on, project codes may be designed to facilitate summaries of research costs on a variety of desired bases. A chemical manufacturer, for example, classifies research projects and summarizes project costs under the categories listed below:

(1) *Sales and Production Service Projects*
  Include activities of laboratories designed to maintain and assist in the normal growth of established products.
  Code Number.
  1. Sales Service.
  2. Quality Control.
  3. Production Service.

EXHIBIT II

CODING SYSTEM FOR SUPPORTING INFORMATION

Employee	John Doe
Code Number	0012
Division	1—Organic and Biochemical Research
Department	3—Microbiological Research
Group and Product	213—Antibiotics: Penicillin
Type of Effort	3—Improvement
Source of Problems	00—Scientific Area

(2) *Research and Development Projects*

Include all activities of laboratories designed to develop new products or to increase sales and profits on present business at an extraordinary rate.

Code Number.

5. Research and Development—Established Products.

6. Research and Development—Related New Products.

7. Research and Development—Unrelated New Products.

Another example from *NAA Research Report No. 29* illustrates the development of additional information and the purpose this information is intended to serve. (See Exhibit II.)

The code number shown in Exhibit II is entered on time sheets filled out by individual laboratory employees. The first six digits in the code (which are pre-printed on time sheets) identify the person who did the work, his division, and his department. The remaining digits (which are filled in by the individual) identify the product group and the item worked on, the purpose (that is, to improve the product), and the origin of the project. The project source code serves as a basis for accounting distribution of costs when projects are carried out as a service to responsibilities outside of the research and development department. This plan for classifying research projects accomplishes the following purposes:

(1) It furnishes, a short-term record to research management, that is, to the department head, to the division head, and to the vice-president responsible for research, on how the effort of the scientific areas is being applied.

(2) It serves as a basis for projecting and preparing new budgets.

(3) It furnishes a long-time record of approximate expense by project.

(4) It furnishes a long-time record of the types of research effort expended.

15

Industrial Research Budgeting

The nature of research must be kept in mind in designing a plan for control of research costs. Unlike manufacturing, neither the precise form of the end-result nor the exact procedures necessary to obtain this result can be predicted with certainty. Except for routine supporting functions, research involves training, skill, and judgment in a high degree. For this reason, reliable standards usually cannot be set for measuring efficiency of research operations as they can for repetitive manufacturing operations. Under these circumstances control over research costs is concerned with the amount and direction of the work to be done rather than with the results obtained.

THE RESEARCH BUDGET

The principal financial control for research activities is the periodic budget. Through the budget, management can control the total amount of money spent for research and it can direct expenditures to make sure that funds are spent in the way management wants them to be spent.

This is accomplished by planning how available funds are to be used and by comparing current expenses with budgets to aid management in charge of research to keep actual expenditures within limits. The research budget is an appropriation type budget in which expense allowances are based upon preplanned activity rather than a flexible budget in which the experienced activity level determines the amount of allowable expense. However, when properly applied, the budget does not restrict research management's judgment as to how its resources can be best used, because individual budget allowances should always be subject to revision—either upward or downward—if new developments indicate that previously made plans should be changed.

Recognition should be given to the fact that the budget is a financial control tool, and not a device to measure the output of research operations. In many respects, budgetary control of research expense is similar to control of advertising expense. While the application of effort can be controlled through the control of expenditures, measurement of results obtained in relation to specific expenditures is usually uncertain and often impossible. Certain goals in the form of new knowledge may underlie the allocation of resources when the budget is prepared, but expenditures are not contingent upon realization of these goals. Budgetary control over research expenses should *not* be confused with budgetary control over variable manufacturing costs, where the amount of allowable expenditure can be based directly on output of a measurable product under standardized conditions.

The scope and objectives of a research program are determined by top management, and policy, once established, usually continues from year to year. Each year the amount to be spent for research is determined by a specific appropriation made by top executive management or the board of directors.

Detailed Budget for Research Expense. In some companies a detailed budget covering projects proposed and facilities to carry out work entailed by these projects is prepared before the annual appropriation for research is made. In other companies, project planning at the annual budget stage is limited to projects to be continued from the prior period with, in addition, broad plans for new projects.

An NAA study of accounting for research and development costs ("Accounting for Research and Development Costs," *Research Report 29*) states that detailed budgeting of research costs generally starts with consideration of personnel and facilities that are expected to be available. These are then tentatively distributed to proposed projects. The reason for this approach is that a qualified scientific and technical staff cannot be expanded or contracted in accord with short-period shifts in research plans. Effective research requires long-range planning and stable employment for personnel. However, outside research organizations can often be used to supplement a company's own research facilities.

Salaries and wages comprise a major share of research costs. The number of employees and corresponding salary and wage schedules constitute source information for determining the amount of salary expense to be budgeted for the coming period.

Costs of ordinary supplies and services consumed in research are usually related to the number of man-hours and can be conveniently budgeted by developing expense rates per man-hour. Separate estimates should be made for projects which will require substantial expenditures for materials, outside services, consultants' fees, or other items. Fixed charges for occupancy of space, depreciation of equipment, apportioned corporate administrative expense, and any other similar expenses are budgeted as annual totals.

Budgeting by Projects.   In some cases the annual research budget is completely built up by projects as well as by source of expense. In other cases capacity for research provided by costs budgeted is only partially assigned to specific projects when the annual budget is prepared. The detail in which project costs are prepared also varies according to nature of the planned projects and practices of the company. Detailed budgeting is desirable when the operations to be performed can be planned in advance and time requirements can be estimated with sufficient reliability to constitute a useful guide. Many product development or application projects fall in this class. On the other hand, projects in the field of "pure" or exploratory research of a broad character cannot be budgeted in detail because no one can predict what work will be necessary or what the outcome may be. In general, as a project moves closer to the stage of commercial application, costs are more closely controlled by pre-established estimates of costs to be incurred.

Detailed estimates of time applied to projects by classes of employees are prepared by research management because this work can be done only by persons who possess an understanding of the technical problems that will be encountered. The accountant assists by translating research plans expressed in man-hours into dollars of research expense. The accountant also applies overhead rates for charging projects with an appropriate share of indirect costs which cannot be identified with individual projects. However, throughout the budgetmaking process, decisions and plans for use of personnel and facilities are a responsibility of management in charge of research, and the accountant's function is to assist management to express these plans in financial terms.

Once the research budget has been prepared, it provides the basis for subsequent control to make sure that previously made plans are carried out. However, as the budget period progresses, research management reviews progress in projects under way and may make revisions in the budget. Unused funds may be shifted from one project to another, new projects introduced, and unpromising projects terminated.

MAINTAINING CURRENT CONTROL

Current control over research costs is concerned with keeping actual expenses in line with expenses budgeted. Reports showing actual expenses to date in comparison with budgeted expenses are needed to guide research management in maintaining control over costs.

The purposes of cost control in its application to research activities should be understood throughout the organization to insure cooperation. These purposes are:

(1) To make sure that the plan expressed in the budget is followed by directing funds into projects of types desired.

(2) To avoid spending research funds on nonproductive or nonresearch activities.

(3) To stimulate an attitude of dollar-consciousness so that

research personnel will attempt to perform as much research as possible for the funds available.

(4) To keep the total spent for research within the limit set by the appropriation for the period.

To reduce the amount spent for research should not be an objective of cost control. On the contrary, the fact that expenditures are substantially less than budgeted is likely to indicate that planned work is not proceeding. If true, managerial attention is needed to prevent loss of profits in the future.

Variances from budget signal deviations from the planned application of funds. They have no significance as a measure of results accomplished by research personnel.

Project budgets are estimates prepared to guide application of funds rather than to set rigid limits to project costs. When actual expenditures approach the amounts estimated, a review of the project should be made. At this time, research management decides whether to recommend an additional appropriation or to discontinue the work. When a project promises a valuable outcome, it is unlikely to be closed because it could not be completed with the initial appropriation.

16
Internal Auditing

Internal Auditing is defined by the Institute of Internal Auditors as "an independent appraisal activity within an organization for the review of operations as a service to management. It is a managerial control which functions by measuring and evaluating the effectiveness of other controls. The objective of internal auditing is to assist all members of management in the effective discharge of their responsibilities by furnishing them with analyses, appraisals, recommendations, and pertinent comments concerning the activities reviewed. The internal auditor is concerned with any phase of business activity where he can be of service to management. This involves going beyond the accounting and financial records to obtain a full understanding of the operations under review.

"The attainment of this overall objective involves such activities as:

- Reviewing and appraising the soundness, adequacy, and application of financial and other operating controls, and promoting effective control at reasonable cost.
- Ascertaining the extent of compliance with established policies, plans, and procedures.
- Ascertaining the extent to which company assets are accounted for and safeguarded from losses of all kinds.
- Ascertaining the reliability of management data developed within the organization.
- Appraising the quality of performance in carrying out assigned responsibilities.
- Recommending operating improvements."

DEVELOPMENT OF INTERNAL AUDITING

Over the years, internal auditing has broadened materially in its objectives and scope. Originally an activity concerned primarily with the protection of cash, later reaching into the area of the verification of accounting documents and records, it is now a managerial control dealing with operations as well as with financial matters. This new concept does not eliminate the valuable and necessary services embodied in the earlier activities of internal auditing—protection of assets and accuracy and propriety of accounting entries. These services are still an important segment of any internal auditing program.

The growth of businesses and the accompanying decentralization of operating responsibility brought a trend toward the recognition and establishment of internal auditing as a distinct function. At the present time, virtually all large business enterprises and many governmental units maintain internal auditing staffs as an essential feature of their management control. This considerably broader field of activity calls for higher qualification standards for internal auditing.

By way of contrast, a survey of internal auditing conducted by the Institute of Internal Auditors revealed that 30% of the respondents indicated that their company did not have an internal audit function in 1957. This is evidence of management's increasing recognition of internal audit as a necessary management control.

In most companies, the constructive accomplishments of the internal auditor in the financial area have lead to the extension of the scope of the internal auditor's responsibility to the operating departments. Some internal auditors cover all areas of their company operations; a majority include such functions as purchasing and sales in their regular audit programs.

OPERATIONAL CONTROLS AND AUDITING

The operational controls that are reviewed and analyzed by the internal auditor include (1) Organization Structure, (2) Procedures, (3) Accounting and Other Records, (4) Reports, and (5) Standards of Performance (such as budgets and standard costs).

The extension of internal auditing to operating departments has led to the use of the term *operational auditing*. Since the operating controls and the techniques of the internal auditor are similar for all departments (both financial and operating), the terms *operational auditing* and *internal auditing* should be considered synonymous.

Audit Procedures.   An internal audit comprises four phases:

(1) *Familiarization*. Here the internal auditor, through discussions with operating personnel, acquaints himself with the objectives and problems of the department, and the manner in which these are met and controlled by departmental management. Familiarization will include a review of procedures which govern the work of the department.

(2) *Verification*. Here the internal auditor examines and tests to learn whether actual operations and assignments of responsibility follow the plans laid down by departmental management.

(3) *Evaluation*. Here the objective is to analyze the findings and to decide whether there appears to be some deficiency in operating controls. For example, the regular departmental reports may not present an adequate picture of operations to management.

(4) *Reporting*. Here the internal auditor reports his findings and makes constructive recommendation where required. An essential of reporting is that the report be discussed with the management of the audited department before formal submission.

LIMITATIONS IN RECOMMENDATION

In certain areas, such as financial control, the internal auditor will be qualified by background and experience to give a definite recommendation for improvement or correction of an unsatisfactory situation. In some operating areas, he may not have sufficient technical background to permit definite recommendation. In such areas, his analysis and study of management controls will be directed to making sure that these controls and his report bring to management attention those situations which may require further study by qualified experts. For example, a physical inspection in the course of an audit of receiving operations might reveal that the receiving department appeared to be unduly congested with received materials. Possible corrective measures might include such measures as: (1) revised material handling; (2) revised production scheduling; (3) revised receiving procedures.

ORGANIZATIONAL RELATIONSHIPS

The scope and recognition accorded to internal auditing in a business are entirely dependent on the delegation of authority from management. The usual trend is for scope and recognition to broaden when the internal auditor demonstrates his ability as a constructive analyst. A statement by the Institute of Internal Auditors reads as follows:

"The organizational status of the internal auditing function and the support accorded to it by management are major determinants of its range and value. The head of the internal auditing function, therefore, should be responsible to an officer whose authority is sufficient to assure both a broad range of audit coverage and the adequate consideration of and effective action on the audit findings and recommendations.

"Objectivity is essential to the audit function. Therefore, an internal auditor should not develop and install procedures, prepare records, or engage in any other acitivity which he would normally review and appraise and which could reasonably be construed to compromise his independence. His objectivity need not be adversely affected, however, by his determination and recommendation of the standards of control to be applied in the development of systems and procedures under his review."

The majority of internal auditors report to a senior operative executive, such as an executive vice president or financial vice president.

The role of a business analyst—a representative of top management—dealing with operating as well as financial affairs, has raised the qualification standards for an internal auditor. His initial qualifications, special training programs, acquaintance with management policies and plans, and knowledge of the detailed operations of many departments help to prepare the internal auditor for higher positions in his company. He gains knowledge of his company at the operating level—and at the same time gains experience in the constructive analysis of managerial controls. These factors combine to result in the use of the internal audit department as an executive training ground. In some companies, service on the internal audit staff for a specific period is preliminary to transfer to line executive positions in operating or financial areas. In a survey conducted by The Institute of Internal Auditors, it was found that 61% of the companies answering used internal auditing as a managerial training ground. This affirmative response was concentrated among the medium- and large-sized organizations surveyed.

RELATIONSHIP WITH PUBLIC ACCOUNTING

Because some of the verification and testing techniques of internal auditing are similar to those of public accounting, there is often an erroneous assumption that there is little difference between these two functions. In fact, the two are complementary, as will be seen by a consideration of the objectives.

The independent public accountant seeks to determine whether or not the financial statements issued by a company are true representations of its financial position—whether data are accurate and accounting nomenclature is proper; whether the statements are the end result of procedures which are generally accepted in accounting circles, and which are consistent with similar previous statements.

The internal auditor, however, is an employee of management. His status and interests are quite different from those of the public accountant. All of his studies are designed to assist the top management of his company by furnishing information as to whether operations are being conducted in accordance with management policies and plans, and whether performance is satisfactory. He is, therefore, an integral and important part of his company's scheme of managerial control.

The internal auditor is concerned not only with the historical accuracy of the statements but with investigating the possible existence of conditions which, if corrected, might result in increased profits or better operation in the year ahead. His activities go beyond the postmortem aspects of operations; they point the way to future improvements.

He is charged with the responsibility for examining and appraising the effectiveness of the operating controls; whether company policies and programs have been followed; and whether operating waste has occurred. Beyond this, the internal auditor relates the controls to the physical operations of his company, makes recommendation for improvement of the business, and covers nonfinancial areas of his business as a regular part of his work.

17

Credit Management

Credit Management is one of the most crucial areas of financial management, for it controls the equivalent of company assets which are made temporarily available to outside interests. The credit manager must integrate internal financial policy and company profit planning with market strategy, the sales effort, and customer development.

It has become a business aphorism that no sale is complete until the money has been collected. The sale itself is only half of the transaction. The credit manager's job is to complete it, by a variety of special techniques and skills, and within a company credit policy which credit management determines, together with the company's other policy-making executives.

DEFINITION

Credit involves three components: an exchange of values, futurity, and trust. It is usually defined as the ability of an individual or enterprise to obtain economic value, on faith, in return for an expected payment of equivalent economic value, usually at some specified future time.

Short-term credit extended by suppliers to commercial buyers for the purchase of goods or services is known as *commercial*, *trade*, or *business* credit. A high proportion of outstanding trade credit is *open-book credit*, appearing as purchase orders and sales invoices. Mutual trust and successful experience are the basis of the wide use and current availability of open-book credit, the primary concern of credit management in business.

SCOPE OF CREDIT MANAGEMENT

Credit transactions, in some form, have probably been a business practice since men first did business with each other. Credit has certainly been part of the American business scene since the early colonists. The Plymouth settlement was financed by a seven-year loan from London merchants. Credit, in part, financed the American Revolution, the extension of the frontier, and later, the nation's industrial growth.

But since World War II, business credit management has become a more precise and imaginative managerial tool for fiscal control, market expansion, customer development, and profit building. Like other business functions, it has changed with the impact of automation and the forces of an increasingly competitive and expanding market.

Credit is a dynamic force in the total business economy. Analysis of U.S. Department of Commerce data indicates that approximately 90% of manufacturing sales, and more than 92% of wholesale sales are credit rather than cash transactions.

Although often overlooked, commercial credit is of immense importance to the economy. At midyear, 1977, the volume of trade accounts receivable outstanding amounted to $361 billion. This total, which was for all corporations (except banks and insurance companies), considerably surpassed the volume of consumer credit (excluding home mortgages) of $196 billion. That businesses rely heavily upon commercial credit for much of their financing is pointed up by the fact that commercial and industrial loans outstanding in our nation's banks in the second quarter of 1977 amounted to $193 billion. Commercial credit is much more widely used than bank credit. Almost every business depends to some extent on commercial credit to meet its needs.

In recent years the growth of commercial credit has been remarkable. It has grown by 75% since 1970. This matches the

75% increase in commercial and industrial loans at banks during the same period.

During recent years manufacturers have invested greater amounts of funds in their receivables as they have extended ever more credit to meet competitive conditions. In many companies, particularly smaller ones, receivables are now the largest single concentration of assets. In the second quarter of 1977, receivables of manufacturers accounted for 16.7% of all corporate assets, but in small companies they accounted for a much larger share. For instance, in manufacturing companies with assets over $1 billion, receivables were 12.6% of total assets in the second quarter of 1977, while for manufacturers with assets under $5 million, the comparable figure was 27.6%. Small companies rely a great deal upon their suppliers for financing.

CREDIT RESPONSIBILITY

The credit management function is handled at a variety of management levels, usually depending on the size of the company. An analysis of the membership of the 41,000-member National Association of Credit Management indicates that 25% of those charged with credit responsibility carry the title of President, Owner, Partner, or Vice President. General Managers and other titled officers account for 19% and credit managers for 40%. In other companies the credit function is sometimes handled by the controller, the office manager, and the branch manager, among others.

POLICIES

Four basic, alternative credit policies are available to business, individually determined in relation to company goals and such specific factors as market, business function, size, and the current state of the economy:

(1) A liberal credit policy with a liberal collection policy.

(2) A liberal credit policy with collection strictly enforced.

(3) A strict credit policy with a liberal collection policy.

(4) A strict credit policy with a strict collection policy.

The first policy offers the advantage of savings in credit administration costs. But it might result in bad debts and slow collections that would more than offset the savings. Few companies would find this policy profitable, but might institute it to attract customers, providing that profit margins could be set high enough to offset potential loss.

A liberal credit policy with strict collection enforcement fills all customer orders but closely follows up on payments. This type of policy is most common in lines which sell relatively small orders of high mark-up, low unit-price goods. Analysis costs are low. But collection costs may be unusually high.

A strict credit policy with a liberal collection policy concentrates on pre-selecting customers who will be good credit risks, but does not exert pressure for payment. This policy assumes that carefully picked customers will tend to pay their bills within or close to terms.

A strict credit and strict collection policy goes one step farther. It pre-selects the most desirable credit accounts, and strictly enforces payment terms. Bad debt losses are minimized. But the detailed analysis of customer risk is expensive, as is the administration of collection effort. Sales potential may also be curtailed.

In practice, most companies will establish credit policies that mix these elements, and will periodically subject any policy to scrutiny in terms of current marketing strategy, economic and industry conditions, and company objectives.

The credit executive's primary function is to maintain the company's cash flow within the company's realistic financial expectations. He does this by checking prospective customers to be sure that they will pay on time, or by calculating the area of marginal risk in which sales can be profitably made.

Successfully selling this "calculated risk" area of business, for most companies, spells the difference between loss or gain at the close of the fiscal year. Most companies must rely on some marginal accounts for business. It is particularly in this vital area that skilled credit strategy can and does materially contribute to company profits.

COLLECTIONS

The best-planned managerial strategy, judgment, and control cannot provide for every eventuality. Sometimes customers don't pay, won't pay, or can't pay. The collection effort, under such circumstances, then becomes of vital importance to both company profits and customer goodwill. In a company operating on a net profit of 5% of sales, it will take $2,000 in new sales to recoup a single charge-off of $100 (omitting the tax factor).

It is normal practice for the Credit Department to be responsible, as well, for the collection function. This becomes a full-time specialization whenever the volume of accounts is large enough to warrant it.

The Sales Department should be informed of the collection effort, since Sales has made the initial contact with the account, and continues this contact through further placement of orders. In some companies, salesmen assist in the collection effort; in others, they are asked to make initial collection contact with a delinquent account, then delegate the later follow up to the Credit Department or collection specialist. In a large company, collections may be the responsibility of the Accounts Receivable Department. This department is the first to know when an account becomes past due. Notification can be made immediately to the Credit Department, treasurer, and others concerned.

Collection techniques are a highly detailed area of special knowledge and skill. From top management's point of view, the results of the many specialized procedures are what count: (1) the collection of delinquent money in full, if possible, (2) the maximum possible collection of money from problem accounts, businesses in difficulty, or bankruptcies, and (3) the maintenance of continued customer goodwill.

Through its collection and credit analysis functions, the Credit Department becomes a major source of information on the company's customers. In the postwar years, practical and imaginative use has increasingly been made of these resources.

To make initial credit approval, the Credit Department has collected customer data directly from the customers themselves or from outside sources such as banks, commercial credit reporting agencies, credit association industry credit groups, and trade payment data interchange services.

Credit records on the customer usually include such minimum essentials as: business history and method of operation, the customer's financial statement and profit-and-loss statement, the amount the customer owes, what and when he has bought, when payments are due, the names of delinquent accounts (with amount and length of time past due), and his payment record among other suppliers.

This information is available to the company for customer analysis and sales research. Particularly in companies with electronic data processing facilities, it is possible to analyze sales by territory size, customer characteristics and demand, customer quality and potential, and market penetration, to name some of the areas to which credit departments now can and do contribute.

In recent years, Credit Management and Sales Management have coordinated their efforts more closely. The credit manager may conduct a credit orientation for the sales staff. If each salesman clearly understands the type of credit accounts that the company considers desirable and that have proved profitable, sales time can be allotted more productively. Accounts which would yield little profit potential can be by-passed, and more time spent on selling the higher-potential, higher-profit customers. Pre-analysis of prospects can be a productive sales function of the credit department.

PERSONNEL

The development of qualified credit management personnel will improve the company's chances of realizing the full potential of the Credit Department. Many of the qualifications are, of course, technical, and can be developed at the credit subordinate level through in-company training programs, outside workshops, executive development courses, and college training. Educational programs of this kind are readily available to every company from the National Association of Credit Management through the correspondence courses of its National Institute of Credit and its Graduate School of Credit and Financial Management, as well as directly from schools and universities when the company is located in areas where these are available.

Technical qualifications for credit management include knowledge of financial analysis, commercial laws under which credit functions, and such usual general management requirements as skill in human relations, organizational ability, and communication techniques.

Research among successful credit executives indicates that personal requirements include: (1) initiative, adaptability, and resourcefulness in meeting new situations; (2) emotional stability to handle customer and internal relations diplomatically and firmly when required; (3) ability to analyze problems thoroughly and constructively; (4) perseverance in handling difficult situations; (5) ingenuity in developing confidential information; (6) fairness in dealing with people; (7) ability to absorb and retain details; and (8) a willingness to take considered risks for profitable company growth and development of sales potential.

PERFORMANCE AND YARDSTICKS

The credit executive's role as financial counselor has had increasing emphasis in recent years. Wise counseling helps strengthen new businesses or those whose condition may have become precarious. He is uniquely qualified to provide financial advice. He knows intimately the financial pattern of many other customers in similar lines of business. Often he has made or obtained operating ratios of the industry. He sees financial trends immediately reflected in the credit department's operation areas, and may recognize these before customers do. In many businesses today, competitive products and services are relatively equal in price and quality, and such personal service as customer counseling can become the deciding factor in the continuance of the seller-customer relationship.

Credit departments share in the preparation of cash flow forecasts through periodic estimates of cash collections from receivables. EDP equipment also enlarges the applications of Credit Department data to over-all company operational analysis and profit planning, Simulation techniques, for example, can project the probable effects of altered selling terms and cash flow, in relationship to such areas as warehousing, distribution, and production scheduling. The results of revisions in basic credit policy can be more precisely predicted in terms of their over-all effect on the dynamics of total company operations.

The effectiveness of the Credit Department is difficult to measure. A number of indices are used by management, of which the principal ones may be listed as follows:

Number of accounts offers an absolute measure, with annual comparisons yielding a rough measure of the company's credit business potential.

Total accounts receivable may be compared with prior years to indicate the extent and pattern of the company's accounts receivable investment.

Volume of credit sales is an indicator of the volume of business approved by the Credit Department.

Total collections, depending on the volume and speed of collections, may reveal a change in the company's financial position.

Proportion of inactive to total accounts may be a measure of the marketing effort and be used to identify, through periodic review, desirable sources of business for sales effort.

Rejection percentage is a ratio of disapproved accounts against total credit applications within any given period, and can indicate the effects of a strict vs. liberal credit policy.

Customer turnover reflects the rate at which customers change, and may lead to a reappraisal of credit and sales policies.

Delinquency percentage, computable in either dollars or numbers of accounts, can be used to analyze the concentration or size of delinquent accounts.

Aging of receivables, by length of time overdue (usually 30, 60, 90 days or more), discloses accounts requiring further review and follow-up.

Average collection period is useful as a complementary indicator in conjunction with the other measures.

Collection percentage is a proportion between amounts collected and amount outstanding during the month, and serves as a composite gauge of changes in the above three measures.

Bad debt loss percentage, for any given period, can be used to check the results of a liberal vs. a strict credit policy and to review the policy in relation to sales objectives.

18
Credit Reporting

Credit reporting agencies provide to business and industry the information needed to reach credit, sales, financial, and general management decisions.

The seller can make his own inquiry. He can talk with people who know the prospective buyer, examine records to determine whether there are any liens or whether assets are pledged, and even go to the buyer himself and ask for figures which will show his financial condition. However, as business has become more complex, sellers have found it quite expensive to make their own investigations. If for example an apparel retailer in Texas orders $300 worth of goods from a New York manufacturer, it becomes prohibitive in cost for the latter to make inquiries at such a distant point, without some form of clearing house for information. Buyers would thus be restricted to purchasing in their own limited areas where they are known. This prompted the establishment of agencies to gather and supply the required information.

DEVELOPMENT OF REPORTING AGENCIES

Credit reporting in the United States received its first impetus in the economic dislocations of the 1830s. Granting credits in those days was a haphazard procedure, and most risks were accepted on a strictly personal assay of character. A trader from the West carried letters of reference from the local banker or clergyman, and his purchases were often limited to the one source of supply where he was known. Terms, nominally at six months, often ran from eighteen months to two years.

It was a period of wasteful plenty, until the demand of the Jackson administration for specie payment on Government lands brought with it a severe punishment of guilty and innocent alike. The withdrawal of specie form normal channels of trade and collapse of the entire banking structure of the country left business prostrate. Lack of a supported money and the resultant lack of credit robbed the axles of trade of an indispensable lubricant. The Government's cure for the mania of land speculation was almost as ruinous as the disease. Small retailers were reduced to the ancient device of barter, and commerce stood still, at least for a year or two, until credit once more relaxed.

Continental practices based on the personal relationship of buyer and seller were outmoded. Business in a vast, expanding nation needed a new framework, one suited to its problems of geography, communication, and climate. Certain wholesale merchants, seeing the frailty of the "reference system" in granting credits, attempted to support their judgments by the employment of traveling reporters either by assuming the entire cost, or through a cooperative arrangement with other merchants. Lewis Tappan, of the firm of Arthur Tappan & Co., silk merchants, was one of these credit-minded executives who saw the necessity of designing a new order out of chaos. Arthur Tappan & Co. had struggled through the travails of insolvency between 1839 and 1841, a condition due first to large inventories and secondly to receivables frozen in sales to country storekeepers.

It was in this atmosphere that The Mercantile Agency (later known as R. G. Dun & Co.) was formed in 1841, "for the purpose of obtaining, in a proper manner, intelligency of the responsibility of merchants visiting the market from different parts of the country to purchase goods from time to time—the same to be imparted with proper limitations and restrictions, to such merchants and others, as may be disposed to patronize the Agency, and become subscribers thereto."

Meanwhile John M. Bradstreet, a Cincinnati retailer who later practiced law, also established the Bradstreet's Improved Commercial Agency. The name was changed later to the Bradstreet

Company which was merged with R. G. Dun & Co. in 1933. The corporate name of the consolidated enterprise was changed to Dun & Bradstreet, Inc.

There are a number of credit reporting agencies, some operating on a national scope, and many more working on a regional or local basis. Their services frequently include rating books and individual reports. The Jewelers Board of Trade provides information and other assistance on credit matters to those dealing in jewelry. The Credit Exchange Inc. provides a credit-checking service to the apparel trades. Lyon Furniture Mercantile Agency publishes the "Lyon Red Book" and supplements. Lumberman's Credit Association, Inc., and Produce Reporter Co. are other examples of agencies providing credit information to their members in specialized lines. In addition there are others which collect and distribute ledger experiences.

Since the widely used business reports and the reference book of Dun & Bradstreet, Inc. are in many ways similar to those of other agencies, the rest of this discussion is based on the Dun & Bradstreet service.

BUSINESS REPORTS

Credit reporters prepare reports on all commercial enterprises listed in the Dun & Bradstreet Reference Book and on some other, non-commercial business. A subscriber contemplating doing business with a concern sends in an inquiry, and a report is sent to him, varying from one to five or six pages, and containing the essential elements needed in making a management or credit decision.

A Summary Section at the beginning, giving the highlights of the report, is followed by a Payments Section which gives a record of the ledger experience of suppliers. Then comes the Financial Section, usually including a balance sheet. The balance sheet figures are normally supplemented by profit-and-loss details, plus information regarding leases, insurance coverage, and other data. Comments by the reporter who prepared the report are then devoted to further explanation of the figures and a description of sales and profits trends. Then follows a section which describes what a concern does, that is how it operates: the lines of merchandise sold or services rendered, price range, class of customers, selling terms, and the like. Finally there is a statement as to the business organization, whether proprietorship, partnership, or corporation, and the business history of the principals of the business.

THE CREDIT REPORTER

The information for the reports is gathered by a trained group of credit reporters or investigators, working from the branch offices in principal cities. In country regions, travelers visit a town and call upon all the commercial enterprises.

The reporter has a number of sources of information open to him. He will generally first make a direct call on the owner or owners of the business. If the business is new, he will inquire as to the background of the owners, what they intend to do, and ask for the source and amount of capital with which they are starting. The reporter will inquire as to how the capital is to be invested, that is how much is planned to go into inventory, how much into fixed assets, and what type of operation is contemplated. If a business has been in existence for some time, he will ask for current financial condition and strive for a description of any material changes which have occurred since the last revision of the report. In addition to such direct interviews, he may call on the banks and suppliers of merchandise, and check court records for liens, mortgages, suits, and judgments.

RATINGS

After the reporter has analyzed the above information, he assigns a *Rating* to the business. This becomes part of the listing in the Reference Book which contains close to three million business listings in the United States and Canada.

The rating presents an over-all evaluation of the credit standing of a business concern. After using a standardized key for ratings in its Reference Book for many years, Dun & Bradstreet adopted a new key to ratings as shown in Exhibit I. Essentially, the new key

EXHIBIT I

Key to Ratings

ESTIMATED FINANCIAL STRENGTH			COMPOSITE CREDIT APPRAISAL			
			HIGH	GOOD	FAIR	LIMITED
5A	$50,000,000	and over	1	2	3	4
4A	$10,000,000 to	49,999,999	1	2	3	4
3A	1,000,000 to	9,999,999	1	2	3	4
2A	750,000 to	999,999	1	2	3	4
1A	500,000 to	749,999	1	2	3	4
BA	300,000 to	499,999	1	2	3	4
BB	200,000 to	299,999	1	2	3	4
CB	125,000 to	199,999	1	2	3	4
CC	75,000 to	124,999	1	2	3	4
DC	50,000 to	74,999	1	2	3	4
DD	35,000 to	49,999	1	2	3	4
EE	20,000 to	34,999	1	2	3	4
FF	10,000 to	19,999	1	2	3	4
GG	5,000 to	9,999	1	2	3	4
HH	Up to	4,999	1	2	3	4

**CLASSIFICATION BASED ON BOTH
ESTIMATED FINANCIAL STRENGTH AND COMPOSITE CREDIT APPRAISAL**

FINANCIAL STRENGTH BRACKET
1 $125,000 and over
2   20,000 to $124,999

When only the numeral (1 or 2) appears, it is an indication that the estimated financial strength, while not definitely classified, is presumed to be within the range of the ($) figures in the corresponding bracket and while the composite credit appraisal cannot be judged precisely, it is believed to be "High" or "Good."

"INV." shown in place of a rating indicates that the report was under investigation at the time of going to press. It has no other significance.

"FB" (Foreign Branch). Indicates that the headquarters of this company is located in a foreign country (including Canada). The written report contains the location of the headquarters.

ABSENCE OF RATING, expressed by two hyphens (--), is not to be construed as unfavorable but signifies circumstances difficult to classify within condensed rating symbols. It suggests the advisability of obtaining a report for additional information.

**EMPLOYEE RANGE DESIGNATIONS IN REPORTS ON NAMES NOT LISTED
IN THE REFERENCE BOOK**

Certain businesses do not lend themselves to a Dun & Bradstreet rating and are not listed in the Reference Book. Information on these names, however, continues to be stored and updated in the D&B Business Information File. Reports are available on such businesses and instead of a rating they carry an Employee Range Designation (ER) which is indicative of size in terms of number of employees. No other significance should be attached.

**KEY TO EMPLOYEE
RANGE DESIGNATIONS**

ER 1	1000 or more	Employees
ER 2	500 - 999	Employees
ER 3	100 - 499	Employees
ER 4	50 - 99	Employees
ER 5	20 - 49	Employees
ER 6	10 - 19	Employees
ER 7	5 - 9	Employees
ER 8	1 - 4	Employees
ER N		Not Available

makes it possible to indicate a number of grades of estimated financial strength up to "over $50,000,000," instead of the former "over $1,000,000," and, to conform to the needs of electronic data processing equipment, eliminates the plus (+) signs in the estimated financial strength rating, and fractions from the composite credit appraisal.

The financial strength of a business is a combination of size and stamina. A good little business, of course, can be a more desirable credit account than a weak big business, but by and large a business becomes stronger as it grows and as the dollar investment in the business increases. Thus the letter envisions relative strength through size.

The number is a *Composite Credit Appraisal*. As shown in the Key to Ratings, there are four credit appraisals: *High, Good, Fair,* and *Limited*. To arrive at what the reporter believes to be the proper appraisal, he forms a judgment based on the following seven credit factors:

Proper organization according to law, and clear identification
   of ownership
Length of time in business
History of management—successful or unsuccessful
Balance of management experience
Financial condition
Trend—going ahead or going backward
Manner of payments

APPLICATION

The Reference Book is a simple and dependable checking tool. A manager has from it the facts to make a Yes, No, or Hold decision.

Credit Departments use it to set up credit lines based on ratings, check new and unsolicited orders, check small and sample orders, make preliminary credit checks, and keep up-to-date with customers' and prospects' businesses.

Purchasing Departments use the Reference Book to locate sources of supply, and to verify credit standing and stability of suppliers.

Sales Departments use it to give salesmen information on accounts before calls are made; to build and revise prospect files; to determine number and quality of outlets; to classify prospects; to revise sales potential estimates; to select prospects in a given area or analyze accounts receivable; and to set up sales objectives.

CHANGE NOTIFICATION

A "Change of Notification" service alerts subscribers on a weekly basis to certain changes that can affect the credit-worthiness of their accounts. The subscriber supplies Dun & Bradstreet with a list of customer names and addresses. Dun & Bradstreet screens these names against the three million U.S. and Canadian commercial businesses in its data bank, which is updated by some 20,000 significant credit changes every week.

The subscriber's names that match or are substantially similar to the names in the data bank are registered for Change Notification service. The subscriber receives a printout "List of Registrations" confirming those names on which Change Notification service will be supplied. This list also contains the so-called D-U-N-S Number, a unique nine-digit identifying number which has many computer uses for identification, for processing bills, purchase orders, market analyses, and the like.

19

Individual Credit and Collections

I—CREDIT BUREAUS

Because of rapid expansion and sophistication of the credit economy, credit bureaus in the United States have attained great importance and professional standing since the end of World War II. Essentially a highly specialized service organization, the credit bureau exists to fill a specific need for retail and professional credit granters in its trade area, and to provide consumers with the advantages of being able to obtain credit rapidly and efficiently. In recent years, the increased used of credit and the mobility of our population have made it essential for credit bureaus to be of more direct and greater service to consumers. For example, a consumer who feels he has a problem with his credit record can discuss the problem with a trained credit bureau interviewer who will aid him in resolving misunderstandings or correcting errors on his record.

The bureau may be privately or merchant-owned. But whatever its business organization, its primary function is to assemble, file, and report antecedent and current credit facts on individuals in order to assist credit granters in determining the worthiness of applicants for credit accommodations.

Formal Definition. A credit bureau has been defined as a central file of information on consumers in a given trade area. More specifically, it can be described as a business organization that systematically collects and files identification data, pay habits, and legal records of consumers in the trade area of a community, and makes factual, impartial reports to interested credit granters.

History.   Members of various guilds in England, and presumably elsewhere in Europe, worked out several informal methods for exchanging data on their respective customers' pay habits. In 1803 the first credit bureau was organized by the merchant tailors of London. Fifty-seven years later, the idea spread to the United States, and a bureau was organized in Brooklyn, New York. From these modest beginnings has grown an industry which today serves retail and professional credit granters and consumers throughout the free world.

MODERN PRACTICE

The consumer credit system is based on the theory that the majority of wage and salary earners are responsible and honorable individuals who can be sold the goods and services they need today on their promise to pay tomorrow. And statistically speaking, this has been borne out. Studies have revealed that approximately 70% of credit users can be sold anything they want on credit and they will pay for it promptly. Another 25% will become slow-pays, usually through no fault of their own, but can be rehabilitated into good risks with competent counseling, understanding, and a little time. The remaining 5% includes those who do not respond well to their credit obligations and, in fact, often avoid payment altogether.

The bureau gathers personal identification and employment data in individual files. Information on consumer pay habits is secured from cooperating credit granters. Information on property ownership or transfer, chattel and real estate mortgages, suits and judgments, liens, marriages, and divorces may be obtained from the public record. The material is held in strictest confidence and released to credit granters and other legitimate users of such information only upon presentation of full identification and statement of a need to know about a consumer's credit history for a legitimate business purpose.

The majority of credit bureaus are members of Associated Credit Bureaus, Inc., the international trade association for credit bureau and collection services industries. The members must abide by policies of the association and the laws and regulations of the various states as well as the Federal Fair Credit Reporting Act which became effective in April, 1971. The major purpose of the FCRA is to require credit bureaus to adopt reasonable procedures regarding the reporting of accurate, relevant, and confidential credit information to protect the privacy of the consumer. The ACB "Crediscope" credit reporting service is in international standard of ethical, top-quality credit reporting.

Privacy.   The consumer's privacy is carefully protected by ACB member credit bureaus. Each individual's credit file contains only items that are pertinent to his or her credit history. The file contains no hearsay or statements of opinion. Every entry is supported by the creditor's ledger entries or other record to which the credit bureau may request verfication at any time.

The consumer has the right to know what his credit bureau file contains, as well as the right to place in the file his own statement of the facts. While Federal law does not require it, ACB policy suggests that ACB members make a written copy of the consumer's file available upon request. According to the Fair Credit Reporting Act, a credit bureau must delete bankruptcy information after fourteen years, and other adverse information after seven years. Some credit bureaus, however, upon completion of the obligations, delete adverse information after a shorter time, according to local policy.

SCOPE

Some idea of the scope of credit bureau operation can be gained from the fact that approximately 1,960 bureaus, located throughout the United States and Canada and in some other countries, hold membership in Credit Reporting Division of Associated Credit Bureaus. These bureaus maintain files on almost everyone who applies for credit in an estimated 50,000 communities.

Written reports, as well as oral reports, are available to credit bureau users. The "Crediscope" Report is the most commonly used. Trade Clearance, Previous Residence, and Mortgage Loan Reports are other types developed.

In addition to providing reports on a local level, ACB member bureaus exchange information for two purposes: (1) to transfer the credit records of individuals who apply for charge accounts in other communities, and (2) to transfer the credit records of those who move to other communities. To facilitate this exchange, the ACB Inter-Bureau Reporting Systems was founded in 1906.

Can people of all nations attain prosperity and a high standard of living through a consumer credit economy? Today this question is being given continuing consideration by government officials, financial experts, and business leaders throughout the free world. In only a few other nations has the growth of the use of personal installment credit begun. In these it is patterned generally after the systems used in the United States.

II—COLLECTION SERVICES

A collection service may be defined as a system of methods and procedures employed to obtain payment of past-due consumer accounts receivable. As our credit economy has expanded over the past several decades, it has become increasingly important for businesses and the professionals to have available a competent, effective third party to continue the collection activities begun by their own staffs. Therefore, a collection office is generally considered an auxiliary arm of the creditor's credit department. The modern collection service must meet exacting professional standards which insure creditor and debtor of ethical and efficient procedures.

In the early stages of the use of consumer credit in the United States, it was found that no set of policies and procedures could be totally effective in eliminating difficulties in collecting money due on accounts receivable. During this period, many collection methods were devised. Some of these were crude and not in keeping with good business practice and good community relations. As a result, professional collection services came into being to serve the needs of the consumer credit community in a businesslike and ethical manner.

MODERN PRACTICE

Today, the collection service is a permanent business organization, adequately financed and properly equipped, under stable management, and staffed with collectors fully trained in approved collection methods. Collection offices may be privately owned or merchant-owned.

Many of these offices hold membership in national and international professional associations which require that members meet the higest possible standards of ethics and business practice. On March 20, 1978, the Federal Fair Debt Collection Practices Act became effective. This is the first Federal law which regulates the activities of third-party debt collectors. The law lists prohibited practices in locating missing consumers and in attempting to collect from them. The right of privacy of personal matters and freedom from harassment are the main features of this law. The Collectrite Service offered by members of the Collection Service Division of Associated Credit Bureaus, Inc., international trade association for credit bureaus and collection services, has become an international standard of ethical service which effectively collects past-due accounts receivable in a fair, unbiased manner. CSD offices offer a full range of service to the business and professional community from precollection services to debtor counselling. The purpose of the latter is to assist consumers who need advice on how to meet their outstanding obligations and to regain their financial stability.

Through ACB, member collection services have access not only to the International Forwarding System, which permits accounts to be forwarded for "Collectrite" service to many parts of the free world, but also to professional training and educational programs which cover both management and staff.

The consumer credit system is based on the premise that every mentally-competent wage earner is capable of assuming full responsibility for his actions. How well-founded this premise is can be determined from the previously quoted statistic that out of every hundred consumer credit users, seventy can be sold anything they want and will pay as agreed; twenty-five will be slow-pays because of some unforeseen business or personal reverse but can be rehabilitated with understanding, competent counsel, and a little time. The remaining 5 include consumers who do not respond well to their credit obligations and, in fact, often avoid payment altogether.

The modern collection service approaches the problem from the viewpoint that those who are slow in paying will pay, given a little assistance, and many of those who are chronically in credit difficulties can be persuaded to pay through patient, sound collection methods. Telephone, mail, and personal contacts with the debtor are all called into play when necessary. How successful such techniques are can be determined from the following figures released by the Associated Credit Bureaus: During the fiscal year, April 1, 1961, through March 31, 1962, members of the Collection Service Division of ACB collected some $88 million. By 1970 the annual total collected was $223,234,000.

Credit granters throughout the United States and Canada, as well as in some other parts of the free world, have recognized that maintaining a collection operation as part of their credit departments is both expensive and time-consuming. They have, therefore, turned to reliable professional collection services for assistance in collecting their past-due accounts receivable. With the ever-increasing use of consumer credit, collection services will continue to grow in importance as an aid in holding credit losses to a minimum, thereby contributing to more economical prices for goods and services sold to consumers.

Index

Index